FAMILY

Poetry about family, from poets
around the world.

Volume 2

Compiled by Robin Barratt

THE POET

A leading international online poetry magazine, recognized for both its themed collections, and its interviews with poets worldwide; looking at their work and their words, and what motivates and inspires them to write.

www.ThePoetMagazine.org

~

FAMILY – Volume 2

Published by THE POET

ISBN: 9798841102304

E: Robin@ThePoetMagazine.org

Cover image and design: Canva
www.Canva.com

Compiled and published for THE POET by:
Robin Barratt Publishing
Affordable Publishing Services

www.RobinBarratt.co.uk

THE POET is sponsored by:

John Johnson – *Poems Over Coffee*
www.PoemsOverCoffee.com

If you would also like to sponsor THE POET, please go to:
www.thepoetmagazine.org/support-us

ALSO FROM THE POET

We produce some of the largest international anthologies on particular themes and topics ever published.

POETRY FOR UKRAINE
CULTURE & IDENTITY: Volumes 1 & 2
ADVERSITY: Volumes 1 & 2
FRIENDS & FRIENDSHIP: Volumes 1 & 2
FAITH: Volumes 1 & 2
CHILDHOOD: Volumes 1 & 2
CHRISTMAS – SPECIAL EDITION
A NEW WORLD - Rethinking our lives post-pandemic.
ON THE ROAD: Volumes 1 & 2
WAR & BATTLE
THE SEASONS
LOVE

NOTE

We have had submissions to *FAMILY* from around the world, and for a number of poets contributing to this collection, English is not their first language. Unlike other poetry platforms and publications, we do not heavily edit a poet's own work (*if we did, it would then not be their own work!*), so please focus on the poet's artistic and creative abilities, their styles, and the messages and meanings of their poems, and not necessarily on grammatical mistakes or translated imperfections.

Promote your book at THE POET ...

You can have a beautifully written poetry collection, but if no one knows about it, no one will buy it! So our new POETRY BOOKS feature is a great way of permanently getting your book in front of potentially thousands of poetry lovers around the world.

- Showcase a selection of up to SIX pieces of poetry from your title (new/previously published).
- The book's synopsis (blurb).
- The book's front cover.
- The author's biography.
- The author's portrait picture.
- The author's website/email/social media details.
- Link through to order from publisher/Amazon.

We will also add your book and link on our FACEBOOK page, on our HOME page, on our BOOKSHELF, and on our POETRY PROFILES pages!

Go to our website and click on POETRY BOOKS for further details:

www.thepoetmagazine.org

CONTENTS

103.	Rich Orloff - USA
105.	Noah Boulay - CANADA / FRANCE
107.	Michelle Morris - ENGLAND / SOUTH AFRICA
109.	Susan Alexander - CANADA
111.	Tonya Lailey - CANADA
113.	Justin Fox - SOUTH AFRICA
119.	Miriam Hurtado Monarres - SLOVENIA
121.	Doerthe Huth - GERMANY
123.	Zorica Bajin Djukanovic - SERBIA
125.	Lois Baer Barr - USA
127.	Tayane de Oliveira - GERMANY / BRAZIL
129.	Djehane Hassouna - USA / EGYPT
131.	Cathy Hailey - USA
133.	Craven L. Sutton - USA
135.	J. J. Steinfeld - CANADA
137.	Maryam Imogen Ghouth - UNITED ARAB EMIRATES
139.	Shakti Pada Mukhopadhyay - INDIA
141.	Bill Cushing - USA
143.	Mathews Mhango - MALAWI
145.	Sanda Ristić-Stojanović - SERBIA
147.	Robert Beck - USA
149.	Amrita Valan - INDIA
151.	Betty Naegele Gundred - USA
153.	Suzan Alparslan - USA
157.	Margaret Clifford- AUSTRALIA
159.	Jean E. Ragual - SINGAPORE / PHILIPPINES
161.	Caila Espiritu - PHILIPPINES / HONG KONG
163.	Stephen Ferrett - SCOTLAND
165.	Ed Ahern - USA
167.	Theresa M. Lapensée - CANADA
169.	Victoria Milescu - ROMANIA
171.	Marilyn Longstaff - ENGLAND
173.	Francey Jo Grossman Kennedy - USA
175.	Aishwariya Laxmi - INDIA
177.	Mariana Mcdonald - USA
179.	TS S. Fulk - SWEDEN / USA
181.	Mary Keating - USA
185.	Bhisma Upreti - NEPAL
187.	Biman Roy - USA / INDIA
189.	Claudia Recinos Seldeen - USA / GUATEMALA
193.	Anamika Nandy - INDIA
195.	Jill Sharon Kimmelman - USA
199.	Emmanuel Chitsanzo Mtema - MALAWI
201.	Anna Dunlap - USA
203.	Alicia Minjarez Ramírez - MEXICO
205.	Dr. Rehmat Changaizi - PAKISTAN

207. Srimayee Gangopadhyay - INDIA
209. Judy Jones Brickner - USA
211. Rose Menyon Heflin - USA
213. Ermira Mitre Kokomani - USA
215. Madhavi Tiwary - KINGDOM OF BAHRAIN / INDIA
217. Zev Torres - USA
221. Acton Bell - USA
223. Shakhzoda Kodirova - UZBEKISTAN

"Family is any group of people closely related by blood or marriage."

Cordelia Hanemann

USA

Cordelia is a writer and artist, and currently co-hosts Summer Poets, a poetry critique group in Raleigh, North Carolina. She has published in *Atlanta Review, Southwestern Review*, and *California Review.* Her poems have won awards and been nominated for Pushcarts. She is now working on a novel.
E: korkimax@gmail.com

WE GREW OLD

We grew old together
as we grew young together
and sad joyous lonely
connected angry amiable
lethargic and energized
we have seen the sun rise
and seen it fall
we have seen the moon wax
and seen it wane
we have driven through snows
and deserts, blinding rains
and glorious sunshine
and sun of all kinds
breezes have blown us
and hurricanes
and we have been inundated
and parched by droughts
we have suffocated in sultry
summers with no air at all
we have celebrated birthdays
anniversaries, mourned losses, death days
we have touched each other
we have spoken in whispers over wine
we have said what is in our hearts
and we have not said what is in our hearts
 we have said what is on our minds
and our minds have been right and wrong
we have drifted in and out
of each others lives
we have shared meals and sleep
nights with no sleep
traditions and travels
and the journey has enriched us
and worn us out
we have prayed together
tried to stay together
we have had our children
together and we have loved and
"we grew old"
we have failed to love
and I am here and you are gone
I think about what we
have been and done together
          and I miss you.

Gabriela Docan
ENGLAND / ROMANIA

Gabriela is a humanist, poet, beauty hunter, nature lover, chronic daydreamer, over thinker and traveller. Originally from Romania, she currently lives in Watford. Her poems have appeared in *Agape Review, MindFull, Stripes, Writer's Egg Magazine, Spillwords.com,* and various themed print anthologies published by The Ravens Quoth Press, Sweetycat Press and Clarendon House Publications.
E: gabriela_docan@yahoo.com
FB: @gabriela.docan.3

SCATTERED ALL OVER THE WORLD

My parents are in Romania - the country
Where they were born and built a life -
Counting the years since their daughters
Went abroad or until they return home.
With unparalleled endurance, they soldier on
Through memories brought back by old photos.

A few other relatives live there too,
Including the maternal grandmother.
She sometimes sits outside, on a chair
In front of her house, under a pear tree
That overlooks her flower garden,
Patient and waiting for a visit or call.

She greets all neighbours passing by,
Checks upon her beloved flowers.
At times, she falls deep into thoughts,
Puffs smoke from cigarettes and sighs:
Sadly, her son returned home from abroad
years ago; not alive, but in a closed casket.

My sister decided to go to France
Where her dreams came true – not overnight,
But after a ludicrously long and laborious journey
Of self-imposed discipline, study, sacrifices,
In her determination to become a doctor -
With a toughness only found in the military.

I went to England more than a decade ago,
Stepped on its soil, embraced its horizons,
Created a new persona that was about to
Speak, think, and dream in this new language
While adopting and adapting to different ways
Of being, seeing, doing, expecting, living.

England is where I joyfully juggled jobs,
Explored, travelled, adventured many places,
Lived, loved, dared, dreamed, and hoped,
Met wonderful people from all over the world,
Lost and found myself a number of times,
then became a wandering wizard of words.

Pallavi Jain
KINGDOM OF BAHRAIN / INDIA

Born and brought up in north India, after completing MPhil in chemistry, Pallavi worked in a national research lab CBRI, and thereafter as an assistant professor in a college in Goa. She now resides in Kingdom of Bahrain. Poetry writing has been her passion from the age of 15. She had participated in events organised by Srinkhala (Bahrain), *Ten news,*(online news channel, India), the PLG (Poetry and Literary Group, Oman), and many more. Her poems have been published in *Gulf Daily News* (Bahrain national newspaper) and online.

E: pallavijain0101@gmail.com
Blog: www. pallavigoa.wordpress.com
FB: @Ybtante
Instagram: @bhoomi_our_land

MY MOTHER

As long as I remember
She was forever smiling
selfless and
sweet
She was Chirpy
and cheery
She will nourish
and nurture her little ones
She won't raise her voice ever
as she was affectionate
and amicable
She made friends wherever she went
As she was likeable
and loveable
She was the binding force of the family
As she was understanding
forgiving
and accommodating
People remember her
even after her passing
As she was mellow
and modest
Now she lives in my heart
As I am her part
She was my first teacher
She was the best preacher
She was perfect
Of her , I am just a speck
My mother my strength
My whole world
I owe my being to her
Before God I bow to her.

Jeanine Stevens
USA

Jeanine studied poetry at U.C. Davis, earned her M.A. at CSU Sacramento, has a doctorate in Education, and is Professor Emerita at American River College. She is the author of *Limberlost and Inheritor* (Future Cycle Press). Her first poetry collection, *Sailing on Milkweed*, was published by Cherry Grove Collections. She is winner of the MacGuffin Poet Hunt, The Stockton Arts Commission Award, The Ekphrasis Prize, and WOMR Cape Cod Community Radio National Poetry Award. *Brief Immensity* won the Finishing Line Press Open Chapbook Award. Her most recent chapbook, *Gertrude Sitting: Portraits of Women*, won The Heartland Review 2020 Chapbook Award. She participated in Literary Lectures sponsored by Poets and Writers. Work has appeared in: *North Dakota Review, Evansville Review, The Kerf, Stoneboat, Rosebud*, and *Chiron Review*. She is also a collage artist, and has exhibited her work in various art galleries.
E: stevensaj@yahoo.com

PANTRY

Not allowed to linger; "Crumbs invite mice."
The only reason I dawdled: the scent
of fresh ground coffee, cinnamon, nutmeg
and the exotic tangerine candle
from a trip to California—
a dream of the future, never lit,
but saved for illegal light during air raids.
Our pantry was a holding place: flour, sugar,
lard and items pickled, canned, preserved,
"Put by," they said; winter's storehouse
when fresh food ran out. The aroma
of exotic spices mingled like those
in russet and orange from an obscure
market in Turkestan. Peaches and pole beans
in glass jars—a staple.
By March, shelves emptied. Then, tins
of sardines, herring, Campbell's
pork and beans sufficed.
When vinegar went bad, a film hovered
at the bottom like a manta ray;
my family called it a "Mother,"
a sign that winter would soon be over.
We looked forward to the first spring salad:
early rattail radish and dandelion greens.

Steven Ray Smith

USA

Steven is the author of *a two minute forty second night* (FutureCycle Press). The book was shortlisted for the Steel Toe Book Award. His poetry has been published in: *The Yale Review, Southwest Review, The Kenyon Review, Slice, Barrow Street, Poet Lore, The Hollins Critic* and others.
E: steven@stevenraysmith.com
W: www.StevenRaySmith.com

FATHER

More than he will talk on the phone
all year, he'll narrow the iris on a single stainless
steel bolt in a box of nickel, because a fastener
that never rusts requires ranking, then separating
for future retrieval, whereas the sum
of hours of all the cognate
voices who can never lose their prerogative
on the mother's fathomless time
can never, by order, be a problem to solve or
not to solve.

Adrienne Stevenson
CANADA

Adrienne is a retired forensic scientist and Pushcart-nominated poet. She writes in many genres, and her poetry has appeared in more than 40 print and online journals and anthologies in Canada, the USA, the UK, and Australia. She is a member of a poetry workshop in Ottawa - active for more than ten years - who have published two collaborative chapbooks. Adrienne also participates in an active fiction critique group. Some of her stories have won prizes in contests held by Capital Crime Writers, Canadian Authors Association and the Ottawa Public Library, with two published in *Byline*. Several non-fiction articles have appeared in *Byline* and *Anglo-Celtic Roots*. She has completed and plans to query an historical novel, *Mirrors & Smoke*.

E: adrienne@magma.ca
Twitter: @ajs4t

MY GREAT-UNCLES

a pair of brothers
picked a pear
pared it
shared it
warm summer juice
tangy sweetness
crunchy flesh

a pair of brothers
accepted the call
dreamed of flight
in fragile kites
soared
roared
crashed to earth

a pair of brothers
RFC cadet
POW ace
mourned in death
glorified as heroes
always remembered

Daun Daemon

USA

Daun teaches scientific communication at North Carolina State University. She began writing poems when she was eight years old, often about cats or friends. Her stories have appeared in: *Flock, Dead Mule School, Literally Stories*, *Delmarva Review,* and others, and she has published poems in a large number of publications including: *Third Wednesday, Typehouse Literary Review, Remington Review, Deep South Magazine, Into the Void, Peeking Cat Literary,* and *Amsterdam Quarterly*. Her poems have twice been nominated for a Pushcart Prize. She is currently at work on a memoir in poetry, as well as short stories inspired by her mother's shop.
E: daundaemon@gmail.com

DIFFERENT DADDIES

my sisters and I had different daddies
they were raised by a man with dreams and ambition
a young and virile man with wiry muscles
sparkly blue eyes, quick wit and ready laugh
he cooed to and cuddled his baby girls
cared for his aged father
built a beauty shop for his lovely wife
began the climb to the executive suite

I would have liked that man
would have loved having him as my daddy
been proud to speak his name at school —
he left by the time my sisters were teens
when I, much younger than they, was in third grade

my daddy was a different man
a drunkard who stumbled through life
gambled away his money, lost jobs
spent months at a go doing nothing, being nothing
spat insults at his righteous mother-in-law
choked his lovely wife as I watched and pleaded
thrashed our dog with the buckle end of his belt

I wanted to like that man
wanted him to be the daddy
he had been for my sisters
the daddy I deserved

he was the daddy I got
so he was the daddy I loved

Allen Ashley
ENGLAND

Allen is an award-winning writer and editor based in London. Recent anthology appearances include: *Musings of the Muses* (Brigids Gate Press, 2022), *Vital Signals* (NewCon Press, 2022), and *No More Heroes* (PS Publishing, 2021). Allen's poetry collection, *Echoes from an Expired Earth,* was published in paperback by Demain Publishing in 2021. Allen works as a creative writing tutor, and is the founder of the advanced S /F group Clockhouse London Writers.
E: allenashley-writer@hotmail.co.uk
W: www.allenashley.com

BIRTHDAY TREAT

Solid cuboid plateau
of stodgy chocolate sponge,
swathed in sweet green icing
with white piping.
Mother - creator of this football-pitch
styled birthday cake - will make sure
I get a generous slice
after I blow out all my candles in one go.

I hardly ever had parties.
Pass the flipping parcel -
all those greedy sods hanging on to it
for seconds, minutes.
like it was a banker's bonus.
Musical chairs:
a free for all fist fight
once the song had stopped.
Some weird preparation for adult conflicts
in clubs and pubs and discos.

So it's my birthday
yet my sister
will somehow contrive
to make it all about her.
She has form on that.
But this candlelit confection,
decorated like a miniature football pitch
most definitely relates to me.
Once again, the consolation of cake.

John Nixon
SWEDEN

John was English, is now Swede-ish, and lives in Gothenburg on the Swedish west coast. He used to teach English to high-school students and adults, but nowadays lives by writing and translating technical and educational texts. In his spare time he blogs and writes poetry, short stories and pieces of novels, and is a member of the on-line writers' group Pens Around the World.

W: www.thesupercargo.com
Instagram: @thesupercargo
Twitter: @thesupercargo

SMOKED

Dad smoked all his life. Preferred Players Navy Cut.
"Players Please!" The ads. "Cool and Sweet!"
I brought him duty-free packs, coming from abroad.
Two hundred coffin-nails in each.
They scented my bag through the cellophane.
Sweet, yes, flowery almost.
How could they smell so foul when he smoked them?

He lit each new fag from the dying embers of the last,
and sat back to suck the smoke deep.
Together in his kitchen we watched *Countdown* on TV through the
fug.
He coughed out his answers while my eyes wept.
I'd go out to the garden to breathe
and nod to neighbours standing in their doorways, cigarettes in hand.

The smell was ingrained in his house,
the wallpaper, his clothes, the upholstery.
It hung on his breath.
Back from visiting the doctor about his feet
(or his stomach, his spine, his knees).
"They want me to give it up," he'd say, indignant.
"But it's my feet, not my lungs."

Then he turned yellow.
We joked he'd been kippered, but it was worse than that.
Pancreatic cancer, four months to live.
"But it's not the cigarettes, is it!"
Yes, of course it's the cigarettes, you damn fool,
I didn't say.
At that stage, what was the point?

He died in October and I flew home for the funeral.
My inheritance, a zippered bag holding his last good suit
and the reek of old cigarette smoke.

Sally Zakariya
USA

Sally's poetry has appeared in 100 publications, and been nominated for the Pushcart Prize. Her publications include: *Something Like a Life, Muslim Wife, The Unknowable Mystery of Other People, Personal Astronomy*, and *When You Escape*. She also edited and designed a poetry anthology titled: *Joys of the Table*.
E: sally.zakariya@gmail.com
Blog: www.butdoesitrhyme.com

FAMILY MATH

Cleaning out cupboards yesterday I found
the cracked clay disc you made when you
were six, a lumpy orange cat painted
on one side and *Mother* on the other. We
had three cats then, one for each of us.

I also found the clothespin doll with its
stiff felt skirt and embroidery cotton hair.
Its tiny face squints up. *The teacher
made me make it*, you told me then
with your little boy's scorn for dolls.

Not to be found: the many balsa planes you
made with Dad to fly on a wing and a rubber
band. They're long gone, all of them, their
tissue-paper bodies tangled in trees like lost
birds or dangling from wires overhead.

This year I'm twice as old as you. This year
you've lived a full half of your life away
from us. Every year the numbers change,
the seesaw totters once again, our end down
and down and your end strongly up.

I don't ask what implacable fulcrum
this family math is balanced on.

Joan McNerney
USA

Joan's poetry is found in many literary magazines including: *Seven Circle Press, Dinner with the Muse, Poet Warriors, Blueline*, and *Halcyon Days*,. As well as four Bright Hills Press anthologies, several *Poppy Road* Journals, and numerous *Poets' Espresso Reviews* have also accepted her work. She has four Best of the Net nominations. Her latest titles are *The Muse in Miniature* and *At Work*.
E: poetryjoan@statetel.com

THE SUBLIMINAL ROOM

That weepy September
marigolds were so full.
Do you remember?

We listened mostly to
Chopin. All October,
leaves mixed with rain,
making streets slippery.
They drop in November
too heavy for trees. Later
growing dry, crumbling and
chased by wind...leaves
now huddle in corners,
reminding me of mice.

I confessed to you
how I loved Russian
poets and waited for
a silent revolution,
revealing my childhood
possessed by rosaries
and nuns chanting Ave,
Ave, Ave Maria. "Your
navel exudes the warmth
of 10,000 suns", you said.

We still live in this
subliminal room.
Jonah did not want to
leave the whale's stomach.
We continue trying to
decipher Chopin. Your
eyes are two bunches of
morning glories.

Sometimes the sky is so violet.
Will we ever live by the
sea, Michael, and eat
carrots? I do not want
my sight to fail. Hurry,
the dew is drying on the
flowers.

Sultana Raza
LUXEMBOURG / INDIA

Of Indian origin, Sultana's poems have appeared in numerous journals including: *Columbia Journal, The New Verse News, London Grip, Classical Poetry Society, spillwords, Poetry24, Dissident Voice*, and *The Peacock Journal*. Her fiction has received an Honourable Mention in *Glimmer Train Review*, and published in *Coldnoon Journal, Szirine, apertura, Entropy*, and *ensemble* (in French). She has read her work in India, Switzerland, France, Luxembourg, England, Ireland, the USA, and at CoNZealand. Her SFF related work has appeared in: *Entropy, Columbia Journal, Star*line, Bewildering Stories, spillwords, Unlikely Stories Mark V, The Peacock Journal*, and *impspired*. More is due to appear in *Antipodean SF*. Her creative non-fiction has appeared in *Literary Yard, countercurrents.org, Litro, impspired, pendemic.ie, Gnarled Oak, Kashmir Times*, and *A Beautiful Space*. Her 100-plus articles (on art, theatre, film, and humanitarian issues) have appeared in English and French. An independent scholar, Sultana has presented many papers related to Romanticism (Keats) and Fantasy (Tolkien) at international conferences.
E: indiewrite@yahoo.com
FB: @sultana.raza.7
Instagram: @sultana.raza.7

RECLUSIVE ALL ROUNDER
Inspired by a cousin.

Though she was somewhat reclusive,
Folks were struck by her sense of humour,
Her laughter, like tiny bells tinkling,
Broad-mindedness, generosity of spirit.

Curiosity filled her with zest for life,
Got on well with young and old,
Despite the huge intellectual satchels
She carried with such ease.

Could easily shake out and hand over
The right bit of info about many different writers
from various eras; carried out deep philosophical conversations
on the roof-tops enveloped by air heavy with
suspended dust, unbearable heat
under the watchful gaze of faraway stars.

Didn't know the winking stars would call her
Back up to them so soon.
Perhaps they wanted to be entertained by her
Musings on so many diverse subjects,
Such as the habits of cats, George Eliot's dresses,
hidden meanings in Plath's obtuse lines, or
the depths of Emily's loneliness, who had no intellectual
equal for thousands of miles around her.

Her songs, which still bring tears
to many eyes on different continents
those who were lucky enough to have heard
her sing live in the confines of her own home,
or those who told us about her many secretive
charitable ventures, the advice she gave freely,
changing lives, and destinies. Her huge paintings,
now mute witnesses to her brilliance,
wishing she'd scrutinize them again for supposed 'flaws'.

Her students, mesmerized by
the drops of knowledge she shed involuntarily
unaware of the vastness of her own grasp of literature,
philosophy, the arts, social disciplines and so on.
A renaissance woman, who was content to stay away
From the merciless limelight, letting her sparse words
scrawled quickly on paper speak for themselves.

Diana Raab, Ph.D.
USA

Diana is an award-winning memoirist, poet, blogger, speaker, the author of ten books, and is a contributor to numerous journals and anthologies. Her two latest books are: *Writing for Bliss: A Seven-Step Plan for Telling Your Story and Transforming Your Life*, and *Writing for Bliss: A Companion Journal*. Her poetry chapbook, *An Imaginary Affair,* is forthcoming in July, 2022 with Finishing Line Press. She blogs for *Psychology Today, Thrive Global, Sixty and Me, Good Men Project*, and *The Wisdom Daily,* and is a frequent guest blogger for various other sites.
E: dianaraab@gmail.com
W: www.dianaraab.com

KINDRED SPIRITS

On the small porch
beneath her bedroom window,
where she took her life,
my grandmother and I
used to sit for hours watching passerbys.

She taught me
the art of people-watching,
inspiring the writer in me.

Now, decades later, I sit
on my own porch and see
how narratives form life's tapestries.

I never got a chance to thank grandma
for her gifts: teaching me to type,
and her nurturing while my parents
worked long hours in their retail store.

No chance to express gratitude
for her teachings:
like how to look pretty wherever I went,
even when putting the garbage,

and to not burn any bridges,
to write my thoughts in a journal,
and to smile when sad,
to be with those who inspire,
and to listen to my heart.

But, in the end, I did get to thank her,
as last week during my pandemic
similar to hers
back early in the twentieth century,

she returned outside my writing studio
as a fluttering hummingbird
to offer more wisdoms and guide me
during my lost moments.

Oh how I wish she can hear me sing
this song of love
like she sang to me
on my childhood porch.

Hussein Habasch
KURDISTAN / GERMANY

Hussein is a poet from Afrin, Kurdistan, currently living in Bonn, Germany. His poems have been translated into English, German, Spanish, French, Chinese, Turkish, Persian, Albanian, Uzbek, Russian, Italian, Bulgarian, Lithuanian, Hungarian, Macedonian, Serbian, Polish and Romanian, and has had his poetry published in a large number of international anthologies. His books include: *Drowning in Roses, Fugitives across Evros River, Higher than Desire and more Delicious than the Gazelle's Flank, Delusions to Salim Barakat, A Flying Angel, No pasarán* (in Spanish), *Copaci Cu Chef* (in Romanian), *Dos Árboles and Tiempos de Guerra* (in Spanish), *Fever of Quince* (in Kurdish), *Peace for Afrin, peace for Kurdistan* (in English and Spanish), *The Red Snow* (in Chinese), *Dead arguing in the corridors* (in Arabic) and *Drunken trees* (in Kurdish). He participated in many international festivals of poetry including: Colombia, Nicaragua, France, Puerto Rico, Mexico, Germany, Romania, Lithuania, Morocco, Ecuador, El Salvador, Kosovo, Macedonia, Costa Rica, Slovenia, China, Taiwan and New York City.
E: habasch70@hotmail.com
FB: @hussein.habasch

IN PRAISE OF MY FATHER
Translated by Sinan Anton

My father, his trousers flowing
His shirt adorned with the scent of earth
His forehead, wide as a field of wheat,
Is still gazing with eyes of love and longing
For the green olive trees
Measuring with the sugar of yearning
The distance between "Shiye" and Bonn
Whose name he knows by heart
He is still surging
Like the river Afrin
Hard, stubborn, and rough
He only fears God
And separation
From another son
He is still repeating his supplications
In his broken Arabic
On the prayer beads
Five times every day
Asking God, a thousand times
Between one bow and another
To protect his children from harm
He is still simple
Bowing to guests
Prayer
And the seedlings in his little orchard
But nothing else
He is still sitting
On his wooden chair
In the courtyard
Speaking to his guests with pride
Listening with pride
Silent with pride
Laughing with pride
Shaking hands with the vast distances in the horizon with pride
He is still comparing
Butterflies and humans
Trees and humans
Love and humans
The sun and humans
Earth and humans

But when he listens
To the news every day on his old radio

Which never leaves his side
Wrinkles and decades of sorrow
Invade his facial features
Yet he mutters: Humans are still so beautiful!

MY MOTHER'S CHANTS

1. The Vision Chant
This morning, my mother was sitting alone at home
Mending my brother Mahmoud's pants
Torn by yesterday's mischief
The needle pierced her finger and warm blood flowed on the thread
The pants were stained and my mother's thoughts were muddled
She swore to my father and the neighbours
That she saw me or my shadow
Or saw me without my shadow passing before her this morning
And when she saw me,
She was so eager; she was confused and was about to hug me
But the needle betrayed her and pierced her finger
Was I really there or was it my mother's heart?

2. The Longing Chant
Mother,
Thirty years... and I am still running with a barefoot heart
Whenever I see a woman wearing a long dress or a white scarf on
her head
I call out to her: mother, mother
Mother!
Thirty years and six thousand miles
Exiled from roses, the sunrise and the face of angels,
Mother's face
Thirty years...
Whenever I write about a woman
Whenever I draw a woman
I find myself writing about my mother
Clothing the image with my mother's colours
Thirty shrouds, thirty graves, thirty...
I am filled with hope and peace of mind
Whenever I lay my head on my mother's chest.

3. The Passion Chant
The inscriptions on the walls of our mud house
The yellow paint on the door
The family picture, carefully hung next to Imam Ali's
The traces of a tattoo on the baking tin

The big quiet stone next to the door,
Always ready to receive guests
Shelves crowded with old newspapers
The lamp, philosophizing with a long luminous tongue
The hanging mat, always ready for prayer
The sacred laugh that brought all this passion and this weariness
Is my mother's laugh.

Carol Seitchik

USA

Carol is the author of the poetry collection, *The Distance From Odessa*, (Atmosphere Press, January, 2021). Her poems have been published in the anthologies: *A Feast of Cape Ann Poets* (Folly Cove Press), *The Practicing Poet* (Terrapin Books), *Poetry Diversified: An Anthology of Human Experience* (Poetry Matters literary prize), *Tide Lines an anthology of Cape Ann Poets* (Rockport Press), and various other journals.
E: carolsei@comcast.net

THE OBIT I NEVER WROTE FOR MY MOM

It has been three years since she was placed
in a shroud of earth. I never wrote an obit □

not in the news of the *SunSentinel*, in the place of sunshine
where she landed after age 50 or the Philadelphia Inquirer

in the place where she landed after marriage or the Jewish
Journal, that covered god. She would not have wanted god-talk

or prayers. I tell you, in her youth, she could have been
a 60s gal, gone for free love and a journey west. Instead,

she settled for the golden aspiration of privilege with little aptitude
for compassion. She rose in the ranks, joined the right clubs, played

the right games, raised two children and in the end, life grew simple
□
broken down to the least common denominator, loneliness.

Mercy wants its say. I think, no one wants to be without identity
like an unopened letter, a life that simply vanished or went
unacknowledged.

So how to atone? As her daughter, the one of her virtues and
wounds,
I can only tell you of her exterior □ she had beauty, customized with
age,

she covered up what was lost. We rarely touched until that day
when I was called to her side and she left so quickly.

I placed my hands on her head, so much came into me. No metaphor
there.
Just mom and me. All language lost, hers and mine. As she would
have it.

Ian Cogntiō
CANADA

Ian is the author of five collections of poetry including *Animusings, Much Adieu about Nothing*, and *Interchange* (a poetry/prose collaboration.) He also co-edited an anthology on the topic of Ageing; *Old Bones & Battered Bookends*, which united poets from across Canada. From 2014 to 2020, Ian was the producer/artistic director of *15 Minutes of Infamy*, a word-craft cabaret based in Nanaimo, British Columbia. .
E: cyberian@telus.net

AS THE CRONE* PLIES

it must be so demoralizing
when you get to the point
where you're waiting to die
where ...
the aches and pains
the disabilities
the sail with no wind
conspire to make each day
a chore, a joyless exercise
in getting up, hobbling
through the hours
and putting a bow
on another day gone by
(if you can even find one
 get those fingers to cooperate)

I realize this is what my mother
faces every blessed day
as she nudges along
at 98, and counting
while we act the 'Cheerleader'
at the pep rally of
"We love you Mom"
trying to give her the incentive
to carry on
to face battle after battle
on a scale of minutiae
we can barely contemplate
as we take our own ableness
for granted

as we try our darndest
not to register our shock
and grief
at her mounting losses

*as per the Wise Woman archetype

Merryn Rutledge, EdD
USA

A widely published poet, Merryn's roots are sunk deep in the American South where her forebears farmed, she spent her early childhood, and where she returned each summer while growing up. Merryn's current poetic interests include exploring both fond memories of that mid-twentieth-century childhood, and the darker sides of southern and family history, including racism. Before returning to poetry-writing, Merryn taught literature and writing, and then founded a leadership development consulting firm. Her essays on leadership have been published in peer-reviewed journals and in books. Merryn also reviews new poetry books.

E: mr@revisions.org
W: www.merrynpoetry.org
Twitter: @Merrynrevisions

BROKEN

Upside down on Grandma's playset
trying to swing the trapeze.
I'm a dolphin diving until
my bent legs slip from the bar.
Hammers behind my face
thump thump. Throb.

Old hen upside down in Grandma's grip,
blood gushing from where her head was
before the cleaver slammed down.
The body jerks,
then wings go limp and splay.
Grandma tosses the head
in the slop bucket for the pigs,
rips out clumps of feathers,
reddish brown like Aunt Veda's hair.

Slumped on the doctor's table,
I watch blood drip drip drip
on my sunsuit.
Nose is broke. His tone is flat.
Like raw hamburger in there.

Back at Grandma's, I lie quietly hurting
while she, Mom and my aunt
tilt the afternoon toward dinner,
when the family tells Grandma
how good the chicken is.
She keeps her *nevermind* face on,
lips clamped same as when
she drives a fence post,
reaches an arm inside Jersey to pull out a calf,
or raises her hoe
to chop off a snake's head like it was a weed.

By the time I'm helping the women cook–
too big for swing sets
and old enough to understand about breasts–
cancer's gone wild inside Grandma's.
Mom and her sisters don't mean for me to hear–
Where Daddy hit her? Aunt Veda sputters.
Not a question, more like rage let loose.
Suddenly I'm upside down again, falling.
Grandma's *nevermind* face–
What throbbed behind it?

Michael Claxton
JAPAN

Born in London, Michael grew up in Europe as a professional musician and has lived in Japan for about 20 years. He has published 14 books of poetry.
E: michael.claxton@i.softbank.jp
W: www.theeyeshaveitalwaysfavourites.tumblr.com
W: www.theeyeshaveitalwaysplaces.tumblr.com
W: www.theeyeshaveitalwaystoo.tumblr.com
W: www.thereisjoyinrepetition.tumblr.com

BRING THE FAMILY

Family (UK) recorded a great song in 1972.
Burlesque
The 'single' was better than the LP version.
The Family (USA) recorded a great song in 1985.
High Fashion
It was nearly all Prince on the record.
'Bring the family', recorded by John Hiatt in 1987,
was an excellent album that resurrected his career.

In my family, everybody was musical.
My aunt, who left us a few years ago at the age of 97
was extremely gifted, educated and experienced, musically,
and had half the alphabet after her name.
Both my brothers still play in bands,
as did I, professionally, for many years
in the swinging sixties and funky seventies.
Here in Tokyo too, sporadically.

When I was small
we sometimes played a card game
at my grandparents' house,
two streets away from ours in London.
The game was called Happy Families.
From my perspective today
and casting no aspersions whatsoever on my wonderful
grandparents,
there was, to say the least, much irony in the name of the game.
But today, my immediate family -
my two brothers, my two wonderful children and my positively
precocious grandson -
all are a source of happiness, pride and love.
Just some of the things a family should have.
I count my blessings.

Emily Braddock
ENGLAND

Emily experiments with writing short stories and poetry alongside her job as a cardiac nurse. Inspired by this work, and contact with other local writers, she enjoys exploring the history and drama of the natural world in her environment. She is particularly interested in the human journey and society's ever-changing face and looks to voice her impressions of culture and community using observations from her experiences living and working in Brazil, UK and Holland. Being born into an eccentric family with many extended branches has influenced and broadened her vision of the world. As well as writing she is an avid reader of poetry, factual and fiction books and enjoys swimming in the Severn Estuary, and lakes and rivers in the area.
E: braddockemily@gmail.com

FIGURE OF EIGHT

I stand at the crossway
Of a figure 8.
A gatherer of family members
A shepherd
A random share
Of genetic and social material.

Circling on my father's side
Drawing boards of architects.
Whose belief's pepper
England's cities.
Straight lines curling
To Europe's mountains
Fields of gold and orange corn
Cows with bells.

Designing for their time.
Minutely changing the world.

My mother's family;
Bohemian
Travel lusty.
Petrol headed.
Bearded, tobacco stained.
Dog eared book corners.
Writing in windowless rooms.
Patriarchal piano, Schubert, Chopin.
Sizzling garlic and onion.
Swims in the glassy sea
At Worthing.
Shafts of sunlight
on fading flowers.
In late afternoon.

My family
Changing the world
by a hairs whisker.
For the next generation.

Gail Grycel
USA

Gail travels solo, wilderness camping out of her pick-up truck, with several pairs of dancing shoes and hiking boots. Her writing responds to the details of place - inner and outer landscape, inspired by the places and experiences of her travels. Her poetry has been included in: *Vermont's PoemCity, The Weekly Avocet, Anthology of Women's Voices* by These Fragile Lilacs Press, *Writers Cafe Magazine, The Medley, S/Tick Magazine*, and Burning House Press. With a passion for building women's confidence, she draws on her long time experience as a custom cabinetmaker to teach woodworking classes to women at HatchSpace community school and woodshop in Brattleboro, Vermont.
E: tbww12@yahoo.com
Blog: www.gailstravel.weebly.com
Instagram: @windleaner

MAKING PAELLA IN AMERICA

Sweet, earthy saffron permeates
shellfish in broth on the pristine stove.
Steam rises, crab and shrimp
bounce in the bubbling boil.

Nostalgia coats the pan's edge,
impregnates tomato, bell pepper,
minced garlic, then parsley.

Believing family immutable,
she labours with stubborn pride,
refusing to smooth her husband's
woundedness into healing.

She stomachs longing in a way
I cannot — beside her,
ghosts of culinary matriarchs
stir the Spanish rice.

Seafood, shelled, drapes
the yellowed rice on plate,
and all that can be heard
around the worn and wooden table
is the unbearable clicking of forks.

Zainab Javid

KINGDOM OF BAHRAIN / PAKISTAN

Zainab has a master's degree in Electronics, and has worked in technical positions in a telecom multinational, but decided to quit her job to be a full-time mother. This is when she discovered her passion for writing. Since then she has self published two children's books, and written a third one which she is hoping to publish. She is also passionate about art, and currently spends her free time dot painting and conducting arts and crafts classes for children.
E: znjavid@yahoo.com
Instagram: @zainabsartdujour

WHAT KIND OF WORLD HAVE I GIVEN YOU?

I tuck you into bed at night,
And watch you sleep so soundly,
Oblivious to all that happens,
Safe in your world completely.

But somewhere else far away,
Blood is shed, a life taken,
A child cries, a mother weeps,
The land of God forsaken.

With time you will begin to learn,
That people lie, cheat and deceive,
They hurt with their words and actions,
And do things you would never believe.

And then that little world of yours,
Will begin to lose its colour,
Your laugh will start to mellow down,
And your trust in others will falter.

What kind of world have I given you?
Worse than the one you were born to,
How did I make it better for you?
Will you make your way through?

And so with a little bit of guilt,
I tuck you in again.
Comforted that you are safe for now,
Away from the sorrow and pain.

Poem part of the Colours of Life, 2022 event held by Bahrain Writer's Circle.

Anne Stewart
USA

Anne received her BA in Literature and History from the University of Minnesota. The natural world is an influence in Anne's writing, particularly since she lives adjacent to the Boundary Water Canoe Area Wilderness (BWCAW) on the USA-Canadian Border, surrounded by Superior National Forest. In the past she wrote mostly for newspapers and periodicals, and published in an eclectic range of genres including a middle-school level textbook, a whimsical picture book in verse for younger children, *I Saw a Moose Today* (Raven Productions, 2007), and *Twelve Objiway Moons* haikus for the Boundary Waters Calendar, 2002. In recent years she has focused more on poetry, and published in *Talking Stick*, the *beloved on the earth* anthology on grief, (Holy Cow Press, 2009), and other venues.
E: astewartu2@gmail.com
W: www.annestewart2.info

INHERITANCE

She told me bible stories,
Ruth, wed to loyalty, her favourite.
In the kitchen she gave me the secret of perfect pie crust,
talked of the blue-sky days of her childhood,
let me roll out the dough. On rainy days,
 through albums of old tin types, we followed the begats
–back to Ruth, perhaps.

In Great Grandmother's rocker,
 or maybe it was Great Great Grandmother's,
she rocked me, talked me through my growing years,
passed on things unspoken, codes
brought from the past: the tilt of the head,
the deft threading of a needle, knotting the thread,
a hobbyhorse ride on her foot.

Time and I put grandmother in a box
and carried her out the door to nurture future ground; I
rock the child and turn the pages of the album,
give rides on my foot,
hold the young hand and feel through me
the flow from past and past and past
to future.

Richard Band
USA

Richard is a librarian and trustee of the Arras Foundation in Lancaster, South Carolina. His work has appeared in numerous literary reviews in the US.
E: rband@comporium.net
FB: @band.richard90

CHILDREN

I have turned from them
to the game on TV,
to yesterday's paper
that must not go unread.
I have stolen from them
to do the things I hear myself
calling me to do,
and yet I remember
her shining face, three years old
lifted to the sky
on the ride at the fair,
fearless
because she knew
I never looked away
until she returned to earth.
And when he scored a goal,
and when he missed the catch,
he knew this too.
For such times perhaps
I'm forgiven the rest.

Dominique Clinckemaillie
SOUTH AFRICA

Dominique is a 22 year-old poet and photographer. Her written works have been published from a young age by the Poetry Association of South Africa, as well in *Love - A Collection of Poetry and Prose*. An only child born to and raised by a Belgian family, she developed a strong love for chocolate and art, and spent most of her childhood writing poems and short stories as a way of elaborating on - and exploring - her world and worlds that she created beyond it. She currently resides on a farm in the mountainous region of the Free State, where she manages an organic farm by day, and studies English literature, journalism and photography by night. Passionate about self-expression and global impact, and driven by the desire to make others feel, deeply understand and believe in themselves and in this intricate human experience, Dominique aspires to one day be a renowned poet, photographer and author.
Instagram: @dom_megane_c

MADAME FIRRE

What an honour -
we share the same blood.
There is so much
you have inspired in me.
My oracle in guidance,
my rescue from chaos,
a life boat in a rough sea.

A teacher of language,
and a teacher of love.
An eternal beacon of hope
from below,
and now, from above.

A true advocate of rules,
proudly of finishing school,
you recite The Book with conviction.
Your devotion
alive in every word.

Your stern
demeanour has its place,
your strict archaic beliefs.
Such kindness in disguise.

A melancholy,
I recall,
a deep longing in your eyes.
Something went missing too soon,
and with it,
profound desire for life.

This,
I do deeply realize,
and so,
your sporadic outbursts
are welcomed with humble grace.
You know who you are,
despite the people you've had to be
in many a dark place.

One simply absorbs,
your limitless capacity for compassion and pain.
Believe me, your

tortured past lights the way,
giving direction.

There is no real end
to what you have given,
let me just say,
with much appreciation.

My dear grandmother,
your legacy is judged.
Not by what you have left,
but by whom I have become.
I am happy to remember
each and every day,
that we share the same blood-
a great honour,
needless to say.

Jude Brigley
WALES

Jude has been a teacher, an editor and a performance poet. She is now writing more for the page. She has a chapbook, *Labours* [Thynks Press], and has contributed to many magazines including; *The Lake, Otherwise Engaged, Scissortail, Ariel Chart* and *Open Skies*.
E: judeteach@icloud.com

MARKINGS

Without my grandsons I would
not have seen wild strawberries

spreading down the lane or
watched the crown of rooks

keep sentinel on the roof
or noticed the light turn

through a day and cast
its net upon the bathroom tiles:

or walked through Celtic fields
at watery early dawn to see

the town awake from silences
of dreams. Without my grandsons,

curious as elves, summer
would have dressed itself

in vain and I would be blunt
with unsharpened eyes.

Nelie Bautista
PHILIPPINES

Nelie is an mentor volunteer to Uplifters, a non-profit organization empowering underprivileged communities with online education and peer coaching to all foreign domestic workers. Her poems *A worker's life,* was published in multilingual translation, *Migration*, *Spring Water* in *Tiger Moth Review*, *Hardship* in the anthology *Adversity,* and *My Daily life* and *Rain* in *Be literate* and on other social platforms.
E: Rannel08.nb@gmail.com
FB: @prettynhelz

YOU ARE THE LIGHT OF OUR HOME

Oh my grandfather why oh why?
it's difficult to say goodbye;
You died without me by your side,
The sadness in my eyes I tried to hide;
I can't believe your immediate demise;
As I watched you with tears in your eyes.

 I feel the suffering from pains we bear;
Let us honour his life with a prayer
Oh sweet grandfather we all loved you;
And the way you love your family true
We pray for you in heaven above;
We send you our smiles with all our love.

You may enjoy the peace have a good rest;
We hope your life in heaven is the best
Your memories are remain in our heart;
And from that place we will not be apart
There will always be fun smiles you create;
Even when you reach gods heavenly gate.

Ginger Dehlinger
USA

Ginger waited until she retired to begin writing. She writes in multiple genres and topics, whatever interests her at the time. Her poetry has appeared in over a dozen journals and anthologies. She has published two novels: *Brute Heart*, set in Oregon, and *Never Done*, in Colorado, and one middle-grade children's book, *The Goose Girl's New Ribbon.* Ginger has won or placed in several writing competitions, including Best Nature Essay in the 2011 Nature of Words contest for Pacific Northwest writers, and first runner-up in T*he Saturday Evening Post*'s 2022 Great American Fiction Contest.
E: gdehlinger@live.com
W: www.gdehlinger.blogspot.com

IN THE SHADOW OF A NAMESAKE

My father named me,
not Elsie after my mother
or Anna after his
but a name without a nest
in either family tree.

'We'll name her Virginia'
he said the day we met,
'but call her Ginger'
(another treeless name).
Mom, still under Daddy's spell,
let it be his call.

I never asked my quiet father,
stern and otherwise detached,
why he christened me so readily.
We never talked much, anyway.
Mom just shrugged;
said she couldn't remember.

I answered to Ginger
long before I learned—
Ginny is a more common derivative,
British gingers have red hair,
the spicy alias is favoured by
strippers, courtesans, filles de joie
(pure irony for vestal Virginia).

Ginger Rogers was a Virginia.
She and Fred were the cat's meow
when I was born.
Mystery solved, I thought,
until I remembered…
Daddy's favourite star was Barbara Stanwyck.

Who, then, was the other Virginia?

Mladenka Perroton-Brekalo
SWITZERLAND / BOSNIA & HERZEGOVINA

Mladenka was born in Sarajevo, Bosnia & Herzegovina. Although she had dreamed of studying literature since her childhood, she ended up becoming a metallurgical engineer at the University of Sarajevo. She taught Metallurgy for several years in a local technical school before the war broke out in her country. She then became involved in humanitarian work - on different continents - before settling in Geneva, where she bow lives. Mladenka works for the Swiss Ministry of Education as an executive and, at the same time, runs a coaching firm for people who live a transition period, whether in their career, or in their private life.

E: perroton.mladenka@gmail.com
FB: @mladenka.perrotonbrekalo

RADICAL LOVE
To my daughters

This is how I love:

I love you when I speak to you in the silence of my nights
While you both are sleeping and me, I am worrying about your
future.

I love you when I cook a soup, a cake,
the ambrosia and nectar
to make your day a good day
To make you strong enough to step in life confidently.

I love you when I am saying it, as many times a day as I can,
Here and there, everywhere,
And when I keep it silent,
While the sky is pulsing against our hearts.

I love you when I am weak, and when I am strong,
When I find your socks on the floor,
Your lipsticks in my bathroom.

I love you when I look at your young bodies bursting out into the
world,
Finding some far resemblance with what used to be mine,
Once upon a time.

I love you pushing the roof of the dark cloud inviting itself in your
concerns about school, and exams, friends and all.
If I am to loose everything,
Meaning my faith in good and in god
My promise to you is to serve a table, soup and cake, with this
ferocious love.

And - when comes my turn –
I will be beaming at both of you,
Ad aeternam,
With a mischief and my blinking heavenly eye
From some far, invisible world.

Tali Cohen Shabtai

USA / ISRAEL

Tali is an international poet with works translated into many languages. She has authored three bilingual volumes of poetry: *Purple Diluted in a Black's Thick* (2007), *Protest* (2012), and *Nine Years From You* (2018). A fourth volume is forthcoming in 2022. Tali began writing poetry at the age of six. Her poems express both the spiritual and physical freedom paradox of exile.

E: chaos.t7772@gmail.com

FB: @tali.cohenshabtai

MOTHER

How much longer are you going to look at me
until I reach the destination you bless
with the Shabbat candles?

A goal that you set for me
whose present and future use
will be absolutely uninhabitable
for me when you clap your hands together as a sign of
thanksgiving.

I told you not to bat
an eyelid towards girls of my age.
The difference revealed to you,
my being differentiated from them, is
the burden of my life, one you're not mentally prepared for,
and certainly not to place me with them in the same
category.

It is beyond me, daughters who satisfy
their mothers' will.
I understand the source of their desire but not
the nature of the ability
to subordinate the good of the individual
for the sake of the "common good," Mother!

I wish you had an alternate daughter and me the same
mother.

We have yet to find such a solution.

Bhuwan Thapaliya
NEPAL

Bhuwan works as an economist, and is the author of four poetry collections. His poems have been published in: *Pendemics Literary Journal, Trouvaille Review, WordCity Literary Journal, Life in Quarantine: Witnessing Global Pandemic Initiative* (Witnessing Global Pandemic is an initiative sponsored by the Poetic Media Lab and the Center for Spatial and Textual Analysis at Stanford University), International Human Rights Art Festival, P*oetry and Covid* (A Project funded by the UK Arts and Humanities Research Council, University of Plymouth, and Nottingham Trent University), *Pandemic Magazine, Valient Scribe, Strong Verse, Jerry Jazz Musician, VOICES* (Education Project), Longfellow Literary Project, and Poets Against the War, among many others. Bhuwan has read his poetry and attended seminars in venues around the world, including South Korea, India, the United States, Thailand, Cambodia, and Nepal.
E: nepalipoet@yahoo.com
FB: @himalayanverses

GRANDDAUGHTER'S EYES

She has lived
the major part of her midlife
in the Psychiatric Hospital
upon the demise of her daughter.
Each year, in a different
state of mental retardment.
Her Doctors say
she is bit fine now
and can go home anytime.
She spread her arms
and gave the nurses
around her a big hug.
They smiled and hopped with joy
but nobody came to take her home.
She looked grimly down
the empty corridor
tilting her head in confusion
and sat down
next to a lame woman
with a child about the age of three
under the shade
of voids
outspread branches
on the dusty marble
of confinement.
After a while,
she heard the chirrup
of birds, looked up and saw
them flying low over head
carrying leaves and little sticks
in their beaks.
She smiled faintly and lowered her head,
and through a window between
the tree trunks, she saw
her two grand daughters
running towards her.
Their face was very bright,
and their eyes were as avid
as that of Navadurga dancers

Anne Mitchell
USA

For Anne, the year 2020 gifted her solitude, a chance to slow down, observe and focus on her poetry. A year of Wild Writing Circles have been both anchor and flame for thoughts to flourish and become poems. Anne's recent work may be found in the *Community Journal* for writers.

E: annemitchell9@icloud.com

DAY ONE IN JOHNS HOPKINS MATERNITY WARD

I run my fingers along the scalloped, frayed photo,
touch the rough edge my father held when he jotted my name
on the back side with his silver Cross pen.

Neat, tight letters that lean right in all caps-
AUGUST 9TH, 1961, 5:09 P.M., 7 LBS. 12 OZ.

Was he awestruck? Did he hold me? Fear me? Or quip
in Captain's lingo, "where'd you sail in from?"

My tiny hands are clenched into fists as though
holding a wee conch, lips pursed for a whisper
through time and faded sepia.

"I blew in here pink, a petal off a Plumeria tree in Palopo,
but once was the dander on the arm of a striped lemur.
I've barebacked the barnacles of a blue whale,
we rode the currents from the Marianas to Monterey Bay.
Permission to come aboard?"

Dad glanced at the African violet, his gift slumped
in the heatwave of August, then at my mother rapt in the magic of
me.
Thoughts shifted to the Orioles,

would they take the lead in the ninth? He had no cigars,
but he could find a cold Schlitz, a radio tuned in to the game
down at the pilot's bar, harbourside.

Neha Bhandarkar
INDIA

Neha is trilingual author and translator. She is columnist in *Marathi* newspaper, and has published 13 books in Marathi, Hindi and English. She is recipient of many prestigious literary awards, and has had her work published in a large number of anthologies, journals, e-Zines and magazines worldwide, and translated in several foreign languages. Her poems and short stories have also been broadcasted on *All India Radio*, *Hindi Radio*, and *Radio France*.
E: nehabhandarkar65@gmail.com

NAME

You, just mine
and I'm yours
I'm yours
and you, just mine ...

But this is just a perception
yours, mine, mutual
but truth is just unaware ...

Perhaps you, all yours
and I'm all mine
just being 'self'
entangled in selfness we are ...

You possess your 'self' enigma
have I too with me? ...

Our bond bound with
an anonymous inclination
clenched with heartstrings
but virtually enigmatic ...
From just both of us ...

Today, wish to question
just this secrecy
What name have you given
to such relationship? ...

Lizzie Jones
WALES

Lizzie is a former chef from Wrexham in North Wales. She started writing as a hobby during the first lockdown, and has had few poems published in *Poetry for Mental Health.* She mainly writes about the hard times that she has suffered due to a abusive father.
E: lizziejayne77@yahoo.com
FB: @lightening.jones

DISAPPEARING MUM

Mum you used to be my best friend, sometimes my only friend,
we used to have so much fun together and many of good laughs too.
You always told me that you were so proud of me,
about the career I chose to do.

You used to tell me that you loved me, every single day,
my reply would always be a great big hug, and say exactly the same.
Now every time I come to visit you, every time is exactly the same,
You look at me vacant and you can barely remember my name.

You have gone to look so frail, your skin is oh so pale,
all this time spent away from you, it's really breaking my heart.
I would give anything,
just for you to have a fresh start.

I don't think you realise what you are saying, Mum!
You are painfully thin and in a world of your own.
I totally understand that you've been through so much,
but seeing you this way is making my world fall apart.

I know, that I'm slowly losing you, but if you go, then I'm coming
too. I just can't imagine my life without you.
I don't recognise the person you've become, But that doesn't matter,
because whatever happens, you'll always be my Mum.
I love you with all my heart.
'Til death do us part.

D. C. Hubbard
GERMANY / USA

Deborah is an American ex-pat who has lived in Germany for most of her adult life. In 2012, she published her debut novel, *The Peace Bridge.* Since then she has written a number of short stories in German which have been published in various anthologies in her adopted homeland. The magazine *ArtAscent* has also published two of her poems. She is a student of history, enjoys playing with language, and loves telling stories that offer insight into the human condition.
E: dchubbardwrites@gmail.com
W: www.dchubbard-writes.com

MEETING YOU

So, this is really you, the one
who's been with me, every step I've taken for months.
Unknown, invisible, yet palpable.

Okay, if you really want to know,
it's not just the last few months either.
It's been much longer.
I've been conjuring you in my subconscious for years,
a mirage, one moment an out-of-focus, distant image.
The next moment, gone.

I longed for your arrival with no idea of who you would be.
Would I even recognize you?

And now, your arrival (an Oscar-worthy performance, by the way)
was not without peril for either of us.

At last, the notion of you has a face
lit by navy blue eyes.
Perfectly formed, but miniature – mouth, nose, ears,
crowned with a hint of blonde fluff.
Fragile arms and legs end with impossibly tiny fingers and toes,
all poised to stretch, to grow.
As though you were a butterfly freshly hatched from its cocoon,
you will unfurl your wings, fly,
seek out lavender and buddleia and drink their nectar.

At last, we've met.

And I, my sweet child, must learn to be your mother.
I shall sit back and watch with delight while you perform
the role of your life.

And should you allow me
to play a bit part in this spectacle,
I shall be forever grateful.

Stephen Kingsnorth
WALES

Stephen has an M.A from Cambridge in English & Religious Studies. He retired to Wales from ministry in the Methodist Church due to Parkinson's Disease. He has had pieces published by on-line poetry sites, printed journals and anthologies, most recently: *The Sweetycat Press, The Parliament Literary Magazine, Mad Swirl, Grand Little Things*, and *Stone Poetry Journal*. He is a nominee for the Pushcart Prize and Best of the Net this year.

E: slkingsnorth@googlemail.com
Blog: www.poetrykingsnorth.wordpress.com

THREE FEET

David Frank, died 18 months, buried Hither Green Cemetery, London.

A graveyard set in Hither Green,
no metric here, nor room to stretch
our bairn contracted to a space,
a span for bridge to other place.
These sods, the clods of earthly turf
for now the resting case, boxed bones,
but hither, green green grass of home.

Gary Grossman
USA

Gary is currently Professor of Animal Ecology at the University of Georgia. He has published over 145 scientific papers on topics ranging from fish ecology, to behaviour and population dynamics. Gary's poems have appeared or are forthcoming in a large number of publications including: *Athens Parent magazine*, *Feh, Verse-Virtual, Poetry Life and Times, Your Daily Poem, Black Poppy Review, Trouvaille Review, MacQueen's Quinterly, Poetry Superhighway, Muddy River Poetry Review, The Knot, Delta Poetry Review, In Your Face, Pearl, Truck, Lilliput Review, Night Roses, Cotton Gin, The Acorn, Blood and Fire Review, Mobius, Poetry Motel* and *Last Stanza Poetry Review*. Essays have appeared in *Alaska Magazine* and *American Angler*, and for 10 years he wrote the "Ask Dr. Trout" column for the latter zine.
E: gdgrossman@gmail.com
W: www.garygrossman.net
W: www.garydavidgrossman.medium.com

ANNA AT 3 1/2 SHOWS AN INTEREST IN FASHION

Your silhouette indents my thigh,
an artist's brush upon my slacks,
slides back and forth, and up and down
as more of lunch is nuzzled clean
upon my pants.

Now blotched with amber, edged in red,
the leavings of a ripened peach,
a dash of green from spinach too,
my wardrobe heralds new couture,
designed with patterns from your plate,
cheek etched shirts and lip glazed pants.

A millennial parent, Ph.D., and a
a four foot napkin, neck to knee.

First published in *Athens Parent Magazine*, 2003.

Lori Levy
USA

Lori's poems have appeared in: *Rattle, Nimrod International Journal, Paterson Literary Review, Agenda, Littoral Magazine*, and numerous other literary journals and anthologies in the USA, the UK, and Israel. Her work has also been published in medical humanities journals, including a hybrid (poetry/prose) piece she co-authored with her father, a physician. One of her poems was read on a program for BBC Radio 4, and her bilingual chapbook, *In the Mood for Orange*, was published in Israel. Lori grew up in Vermont, lived in Israel for 16 years, spent several months in Panama, but now lives with her extended family in Los Angeles.
E: avilori@yahoo.com
Instagram: @mymomspoem

WHAT DID YOU SAY?

I don't know how to help
my ageing parents. I want to lighten
their lives. Brighten the space
between one meal and the next.
But here I am on this visit,
a repeater of words. A translator of sorts.
No French romancing the pink of my tongue,
no quick-tempoed Spanish flamencoing my lips,
just English to English as I sit between them,
telling him what she said and her what he said.
I open wide, try not to garble or mangle,
rowing us forward, past the whats
that pop up like rocks, blocking the stream.
His hearing aid is good, but nothing like the magic
promised in the ads, especially when she forgets
to face him when she speaks. She hears,
but doesn't always listen the first time—
or understand his new voice,
softened, strained by Parkinson's.

One night we, their family, take them out to eat.
It's their 68th anniversary, and he—this man who
can't see well, hear well, walk well—
gets up to speak at the end of the meal,
wishes us all a marriage like theirs. A toast
to what works: a kiss in the morning, a kiss at night,
an expression of love goes a long way.
I raise my glass, laughing at myself.
Who said they need a translator?
Now I want to be a songcatcher
who gathers and records what flows between them:
the melodies, harmonies, lyrics of their love.

Anne Marie Corrigan
CANADA / REPUBLIC OF IRELAND

Anne is an Irish writer with a Masters in Italian Literature from University College Cork, Ireland and a Masters in Journalism from the University of British Columbia, Canada. She was writer and managing editor at *Alive Magazine*, and writer and editor for various science and engineering departments at UBC. Her work has appeared, or is forthcoming, in: *Subterranean Blue Poetry, Alive Magazine, The Exchanger, The Thunderbird Magazine, In Dublin Magazine*, and *Orato*. Alongside her love of poetry, Anne Marie has also completed her first book of fiction titled: *The Cause.*
E: annemarie@annemariecorrigan.com
W: www.annemariecorrigan.com

THE DEFLATED PURSE OF DREAMS

For Mother

"The bank is not my friend,"
You say
As you pluck silver from copper
Out of the wasteland
Of your deflated purse of dreams
Yet, just yesterday you
Were blushed and
Swollen,
With songs
With poems he whispered into your dawn-tinted ear
Swollen,
With plump and golden plums he fed you
Picked from the fruiting tree by the stone wall
Swollen,
With the promise of babies in your belly
Now born
Today, it is cold and you are no longer credit worthy
You place the worthiest coins
In an empty matchbox
That you wrap with brown paper
Addressed to the manager
Who loaned money
With a smile
For the hearth
The orchard
The claw-footed tub
For the home, that was lost
The dreams he spilled
On to bar counters
But still you love
Lividly
The heart
That startled you
From light to night
The eyes, the soul, the mouth
That drank and drank and drank
The gasping shreds
Of your hope, dignity and desire

Durga Prasad Panda
INDIA

Durga serves the Government of India as a senior Statistician. He is a bilingual poet and critic whose works have appeared in journals including: *Debonair, Gentleman, Indian Literature, the little magazine, Sunstone* (USA), *New Quest, Stag Hill Literary Journal* (UK), *Outlook* and others across India and abroad. His poems have been anthologized thrice in British Council's *Poetry India*. His book reviews have appeared in *Indian Literature, the little magazine* and *Outlook*. His poems have been included in the *Yearbook of Indian Poetry in English 2020-21, Shape of a Poem: Red River Book of Contemporary Erotic Poetry, Witness: The Red River Book of Poetry of Dissen*t. He has attended several symposiums and readings, and read his poetry in the prestigious 39th World Congress of Poets. He has also edited a Reader on the life and works of eminent poet Jayanta Mahapatra for the Sahitya Akademi (India).
E: durgaprasad2270@gmail.com

FAMILY PORTRAIT

Father, a renowned vet
loved animals
more than anything else in life.

To win his love
mother turned herself
into a meek goat.

And resigned herself
into a vague darkness
for the rest of her life.

From an early age
my sister mastered the art
of barking like a bitch.

While I grew up
to be a raging Bull
gone berserk

in the crowded street.

First published *the little magazine*, *Vol. VI issue 1-2*, (2005).

Jenelyn Leyble
SINGAPORE / PHILIPPINES

Jenelyn is a Filipino domestic worker and caregiver to a stroke patient in Singapore. She has had a passion for writing since she was young. As part of Migrant Writers of Singapore, through literature, she helps others cope with life's challenges. Her poetry has been published in *Poetry Planet* and *Passion for Poetry*.
E: jenelynleyble@yahoo.com

MY FAMILY, MY EVERYTHING

I came from a poor family rich with values and abundance in love
We always fight the wrong to be right
Where misunderstanding leads to forgiveness
My siblings are my supporter but sometimes my biggest competitor
My father is a ruler but to my mother he is a follower
My mother is wise sometimes being fooled by us
My family is my weakness and my strength
Our bittersweet memories makes us stronger
When everyone depends on you
Sometimes I need to be cruel to be kind
But deep down, I'm really shallow person
I must lead in order to follow
This is only a beginning of the end
Hold on, stay strong and keep fighting.

Bill Cox
SCOTLAND

Bill was born and bred in 'the Granite City' of Aberdeen, where he still lives. Bill enjoyed creative writing when at school, but - as the cliché goes - life got in the way and it was only in his forties, after taking an online course, that he returned to his teenage passion. He now writes for the sheer enjoyment of it, which is just as well as no-one seems willing to pay him to do it. He dabbles mainly in poetry and short fiction, as he hasn't built up the stamina yet to write anything longer. One day, though, he plans to gather his strength and write a book that will set the publishing world alight. In the meantime he satisfies himself with composing bawdy limericks in his head.
E: malphesius@yahoo.com
Blog: www.northeastnotesblog.wordpress.com

THREADS

In Glen Moriston, in the Highland village of Dalchreichart,
There is a cottage that used to be the Glen's Post Office.
That's where my mother was born.
In Aberdeen's Frederick Street, there is a memory
Of the brick-faced tenements that used to line the road.
That's where my father was born.
Two disparate threads, miles and years apart,
Yet pulled and sewn together,
To make a family.

Jayne Jaudon Ferrer
USA

In love with words since learning to read at age four, Jayne wrote her first story at six, earned her first byline at nine, and has been writing ever since. The author of seven books, her work has appeared in publications ranging from *Boca Raton Magazine* to *Christian Parenting Today.* She is the founder and host of *YourDailyPoem.com* a website designed to share the pleasure and diversity of poetry with those who are sceptical. During the course of her writing career, Jayne has been a radio continuity director, advertising copywriter, newspaper columnist, magazine editor, public relations coordinator, freelance journalist, and creative director. She has interviewed movie stars, judged contests, produced plays, scripted everything from nuclear power plant videos to beauty pageants, and even developed a few political campaign slogans.
W: www.JayneJaudonFerrer.com
W: www.YourDailyPoem.com

RED RIDING HOOD REVISITED

All the things my grandmother was not,
I will be for your daughter.
I will tease her with sprigs of dandelion
in the springtime,
tempt her with ripe red melons
in the summer sun,
laugh with her in the languid blaze
of autumn,
cherish her warmth in the starkness
of winter's chill.
We will have secrets,
she and I.
About cookies
and boyfriends,
lipsticks
and lollipops,
late nights,
early mornings,
and love.
I will wipe away her freckles
with the milky mist of twilight;
she will wipe away my age spots
with the dew.
Together, we will
fret about,
forage through, and
feast upon life
from
one end
to the other.

First published *Dancing with My Daughter: Poems of Love, Wisdom & Dreams* (Loyola Press, 2004).

Pinny Bulman
USA

Pinny is a lifelong New Yorker, raised in Washington Heights and currently residing in the Bronx. He is a Bronx Council on the Arts BRIO award-winning poet, and has been winner of the Poets of NYC Contest, recipient of several ADR Poetry Awards, and a finalist for the Raynes Poetry Prize. His poems have appeared in anthologies such as *Escape Wheel* (great weather for MEDIA), and were published in Korean translation for *Bridging the Waters III* (Korean Expatriate Literature & Cross-Cultural Communications). Pinny's poetry has also appeared in a variety of other literary publications including: *The London Reader, Muddy River Poetry Review, Artemis, Pressenza International, Red Paint Hill*, and *Poetry Quarterly*.
E: pinnybulman@gmail.com

HAVDALAH

whoever donated
the silver modernist spice holder
could not have imagined
the way my dad
could make it look
like a hungry space alien
opening and
closing its clove-filled mouth
with a ridiculous whispered growl daring me
to keep a straight face
in front of the congregants
as i sang the start to each week
with choked back
laughter.

Rich Orloff
USA

Rich's short plays have had over 2000 productions on six continents - and a staged reading in Antarctica. His poetry cycle for performance, *Blessings from the Pandemic,* has been produced by theatres, schools, churches and synagogues, was published by TRW Plays. During the year until the pandemic struck, Rich travelled around the United States performing his one-person show, *It's a Beautiful Wound*, about his experience in underground, psychedelic-assisted therapy. Primarily a playwright, *The New York Times* called his play *Big Boys* "rip-roaringly funny", and named *Funny as a Crutch* a Critic's Pick.

E: richplays@gmail.com
W: www.richorloff.com
W: www.trwplays.com

MESSAGE FROM MY GRANDMOTHER

I worry about you
Worrying about you is my joy
And my job
It fills my days even since my life has ended

Have you forgotten all the quiet gifts I gave you
The sensory pleasures of a challah
The serene contentment of a walk
The acceptance of ageing
Gratitude for even the smallest thing

Your parents were fools
But they treated me kindly
They gave me respect
I wish they had given you more

Never forget my tranquil eyes
Or that I left Belarus in the middle of the night
With my husband and four small children
Not only because our lives were so dire
But because we had hope

I sold potatoes door-to-door to survive
I stretched each penny as far as I could
For years I owned one dress
And I was deeply in love

Let me be your angel of comfort
Rest your head on my wings
Stop wasting time trying to please me
You succeeded the day you were born

Commissioned for *"The Yizkor Project"* by Temple Sinai in Toronto, Canada.

Noah Boulay
CANADA / FRANCE

Noah is a prospective novelist and amateur writer with interest in many genres, including mystery, science fiction and fantasy. He was born in France, and was raised in Canada. He has an interest in anthropology and mythology, and keeps a writing philosophy of limiting the purple prose, at times.

E: noahboulay2003@gmail.com

ERUDITE ÉTUDE

how must it be now, to watch?
      you've done all you can, all you could
      for all these years, so now only comes--
how must it have been then, to prepare?
      you had two, twins like you were
      then again, you weren't so hairy.
how must it have been, for such an erudite woman?
      you watched your children play in the yard
      you learned to see everything, from rocks to cars
      you started with one, and became 'mom' to her and him.
so again, how must it be now?
      -to know that your children are leaving the nest?
      his étude and her erudite ambitions has only just begun.

Michelle Morris
ENGLAND / SOUTH AFRICA

Michelle is a South African and British writer based in Paignton, a seaside town on the coast of Tor Bay in Devon. She has been writing uplifting, inspiring and thought-provoking poetry all her life, and has been published in a number of poetry anthologies.
E: morrismichelle4@gmail.com
Instagram: @michellemorrispoet
Twitter: @MichellePoet

DEAR DAD

Dear Dad,
It's me, your long lost daughter.
I'm the one you gave away,
To keep your life in order.

I forgive you.
I understand how life is.
So full of complications
Of what it means to live.

I understand you,
Even though we never met.
You couldn't show your weakness,
Even on your deathbed.

I wish you well,
No matter where you are.
I hope that you've found peace
With God's blessings and His love.

Susan Alexander

CANADA

Susan is a poet and writer living in British Columbia on Nexwlélexm/Bowen Island, the traditional and unceded territory of the Squamish people. Susan's work has appeared in anthologies and literary magazines throughout Canada, the US and the UK. She is the author of two collections of poems from Thistledown Press: *Nothing You Can Carry* (2020), and *The Dance Floor Tilts* (2017). Her suite of poems called *Vigil* won the 2019 Mitchell Prize for Faith and Poetry, while some of her other work has received the Vancouver Writers Fest and Short Grain awards.
Instagram: @alexasusander

NEWS OF DEATH

My sister's voice sounds strained –
is this a good time to talk?

That's when I leave my body.

Up and up I go
through the ceiling onto the roof.
The strait gleams at the horizon
while across the sky clouds scud
in slants of dark and darker.
Here there is
only mist and wind,
spaces between rain.

Down below
the silent movie plays
on a shrinking screen,
wet face with white lips,
finger-tangled hair.
Small children swirl
like water spouts.

Cut strings, and the ocean
floods the tiny room
where a form eddies
amongst barnacles.

A body underwater is all anemone,

arms sweep red-tipped
in tidal drag until
flick and shrink,
it hides inside itself.

Tonya Lailey
CANADA

Tonya grew up on a farm in Niagara-on-the-Lake, Ontario, and now lives in Calgary. Tonya works in the wine trade. She also writes fiction, essays and poetry. Most recently, her poetry has appeared in *FreeFall magazine, Rattle, IceFloe Press* and *Bindweed Magazine's Midsummer Madness 2022* issue. In May, 2022, Tonya completed her MFA in creative writing at the University of British Columbia.
E: tonyalailey@gmail.com
Facebook: @laileyt

MY GRANDMOTHER RUTH

I find her at the kitchen table,
the kind that shines without polish,
after 50 years,
chair backs that curl.

Every morning the same breakfast -
banana over bran
on shredded wheat, on yogurt,
baker's yeast by the bottle, shaken.

Orange juice in a card playing glass -
hearts faded by dishwasher cycles,
lecithin dealt in,
for peace of mind.

Dentures that clomp
the morning mash
and the same stretch-smack
a wet dough makes.

In "the shop", already,
where once hung meat,
my grandfather, too, keeps his regimen -
white rum by the bottle, poured.

I suppose it isn't unusual, in those days,
in Milford, in Nova Scotia,
to find the serenity prayer,
on a kitchen wall,
in needlepoint.

My parents occasionally call me Ruth -
say how much I'm like her,
that I have her nose.

Justin Fox
SOUTH AFRICA

Justin is an award-winning photojournalist, editor and author of more than 20 books. He was a Rhodes Scholar and received a doctorate in English from Oxford University, after which he was a research fellow at the University of Cape Town, where he taught part-time for two decades. His books have been published in South Africa, the UK, the USA, Holland and France. Recent works include: *The Marginal Safari* (2010), *Whoever Fears the Sea* (2014), *The Impossible Five* (2015), and a poetry collection, *Beat Routes* (2021). His latest novel, *The Cape Raider* (2021), is a World War II adventure set in South Africa.
E: justinfoxafrica@gmail.com
FB: @justin.fox.520

THE GRAND TOUR
(June to October 1973)

Map of the world, crayons, a plastic plane
to track our course from south to north,
we rumble through a blue-black sky
and reel across the African night,
just Mommy and Daddy and me
on the adventure of a life.

Tall red men with tall furry hats and prickly guns
where Christopher Robin went down with Alice
near a Piccadilly flat with miracle telly
that's small and black-and-white and fuzzy
but beams movies, just like in the movies,
so I won't go outside to play
lest I miss something nice,
like cartoons.

Wedding bells for Lonka in a mossy Cambridge
of old stone buildings piled like sandcastles
and flat blunt boats with long paddling poles
and Pedro falling in the water with a plop;
then lovely Lonka with doily on her head
singing amens and me in scratchy sailor suit;
a shaggy dog, a horse, a cathedral perhaps.

Now to Paris with Grethe in belly bottoms
and clodhopper shoes as tall as Eiffel's tower,
it's Bastille Day along a Champs-Élysées
of gay tricolours hung from every tree and
armoured cars rolling grumbly past
with me on Daddy's shoulders
pointing a paper periscope
above the heads of all the Frogs.

Then misted blurring Dusseldorf streets
and whizzy autobahns in the rain
to Helmut's mystical *alte Mühle*
gingerbread mill set in a forest deep
on the Moselle where up the creaky stairs
our lofty beds are perched and waterwheels
go splish-splash beside our leafy ears.

South we drive to Pyrmont's castle
flapping with flags and pointed towers,

114

scaredy dungeons and suits of armour,
then further down the mud-brown river
past rows of churches Daddy thinks
'important', for what I do not know,
but cheeky cherubs and lots of gold to
Vierzehnheiligen Cathedral where twin Tintin
rockets are stuck together and painted yellow.

We're dragged along to Munich's stadium,
a tall hobgoblin tent where Jewish athletes
were executed by the Nazties or something,
then round Vienna's ring-a-ring-a-road and
down to pretty Salzburg where Mozart's balls
taste chocolate-yum in silver foils and Mommy
tries so hard to make me like the stringy music:
a little blond boy, a silly wig, a boring violin.

Venice is the best city in the world by far
with canals, vaporettos and crying gondolas,
piazzas where we sit for days with ice-creams
and pooing pigeons swirl like fighter planes;
Daddy leads me up a twirling tower to see
two bronze-green giants clang the hour
with meaty mallets that send a shudder
through me, San Marco and all Venezia.

Passing Bologna, home of my favourite spaghetti
(but not the parmy jama cheese that pongs)
to Florence where Daddy once sat atop his tank
listening to guns and screaming in the war
'cause people had been bad I think,
and 14-fingered San Gimignano
whose skyscrapers look like new
but are, in fact, mid evil.

At last we reach the Internal City where Revie
waits with long blond hair, guitar and tan
in Esther's creaky flat on Largo dei Librari;
our sticky days are filled with fountains into
which we toss our penny's worth in lira and
olive boys on scooters whirl round Navona
with swimming horse and underfed Obelix;
gardens for Africa, Italian steps, rugby-ball domes and
a colossal stadium where Daniel got eaten by the lions.

I ride the Acropolis on Daddy's shoulders because

it's hellish hot and my legs are shot from too much ruin,
to Piraeus for a ferry voyage across a white-horsed Aegean
where Greeks vomit non stop and we hold the upper deck
to a Patmos harbour lit with grapefruit moon and water stars;
a donkey ride, a dark house, the smell of leather and basil
never ever to be forgotten all my livelong days and
in the morning shutters swing open to a boyhood paradise
of white-white houses, cobbledy lanes, a fortress monastery
and the cave where John wrote letters to God about a revolution.

Each morning we take the bus down a mountain to the port,
with passengers singing lustily along to 'Maria me ta kitrina,'
where Zorba's boat is ready to chug us to his beach
of pebbles, dry-stone walls, olive groves and us all
blond and bronzed and basking under a Grecian sun;
remember that cottage in a cove reached only by caïque,
the vine pergola, fig trees, the yucky yoghurt and honey
then a swim in water so glassy see-through green
you could peer past pinky feet to the bottom's bottom.

A night ferry straight from Fellini's *Amarcord* (I later understand)
sailing down a dream-drenched sea to volcanic Santorini and
filling a tiny head with nautical flotsam that will never leave;
a moaning foghorn, a transfer into boats in deep water
then puttering towards that silent cliff-bound cove,
a line of donkeys waiting on the shore
to spirit us up high to our village in the sky:
that's why,
you see,
that's why.

The daily mule trek to the beach, an island volcano
where we peep over steamy lip to the broiling bowels
then smear ourselves with lava mud for Mommy's photo;
the nightly tavern with Sofia's kleftiko and tzatziki,
her moussaka, dolmades and nut-sweet baklava,
the broad black bay far below bobbing with boats,
a violin's wail, the sharp snap of bouzouki strings
and the old men of the village, arms entwined,
dancing low and slow to a Cycladic refrain.

That island of the lonely chapel,
thin its tolling bell,
a tiny monk sits by its side,
white beard, black robes,
blue beads that feed remembering fingers;

our caïque glides closer over broccoli water and
emboldened I
leap from its bows to swim for shore;
Daddy splashes in behind and follows me,
long timeless strokes,
warm buoyant water;
perhaps I'll never stop swimming this swim
towards that rock enchantment,
for I am six, and I am a man,
and Dad is right behind me.

Miriam Hurtado Monarres
SLOVENIA

Miriam is a 29-year-old Doctoral student of Sociology at the University of Ljubljana, and works as a Researcher of Social Sciences at the same University. She has published and co-authored research papers and stories in Slovenian print media, and her poetry has been translated into Spanish and English, and published in Peru (*Revista Kametsa*), El Salvador (*Revista Culturel*), and Slovenia (*The Englist*). She participated in the 3rd San Salvador meeting, hosted by Revista Culturel where she presented her poems in Slovene and Spanish. She is also the co-editor of the Slovene literary magazine *Literaven.com,* which connects the Slovene and Hispanic literary worlds.
E: miriam.hurtadomonarres@gmail.com
Instagram: @miriamc4

MY FAMILY

Between what I think
And what I feel is me.

A human entity of hope
A descendant of dreams,
     A childlike innocence
     With a catlike curiosity,
Always running free
Jumping at every tree.

And then there is you
Who is just like me,
     My dear brother
     My lovely sister
Just as innocent and free,
Climbing trees with me.

Between what I think
And what I feel is me,
     But all around me
     Is my family
Its name is known to all
As the human world.

Doerthe Huth
GERMANY

Doerthe's first collection of poems and essays in English appeared in 2022, titled: *The Fragility of Moments*. She is a member of the German Writers' Association.
W: doerthe-huth.jimdosite.com
FB: @DoertheHuth
Twitter: @DoertheHuth
Amazon author's page: www.amazon.de/-/e/B00458KTCC

WEAVING THE MOMENT

They are with me.
Each of my cells carry
their building blocks.
We are tethered by fine cobwebs
that weave the moment.

This network spreads its wings
and lets the wind of the past
carry into my future.

Threads as strong as death,
nevertheless, light and elastic.
A natural construct
that provides security
but is not invulnerable.

When I don't want to live up
to expectations of others,
it becomes a tensile test.
I need to be careful
not to fall through loose ends
or tangle myself in a sticky catch net.

In those moments
I have to remind myself
who I am without all these
woven goods of my ancestors
and that I prefer to weave with words.

Zorica Bajin Djukanovic
SERBIA

Zorica graduated from the Faculty of Philology of Belgrade University, the Department of Yugoslav Literature. She writes poetry, prose and literature for the young, and has published a total of 17 books including the collections of poetry: *Blood Clot* (1994), and *Lining* (1999), the short story collections *Hotel Philosopher* (2003) and *Said King Of Sunshades* (2009), and the following collections of poetry for young people: *Wizard* (1999), *Tiny Box For A Firefly* (2010), *Summer Day* (2014) and *Brief Love Poems* (2017). Her poetry and prose have been translated into Russian, English, Dutch, Rumanian, Ruthenian and Macedonian, and her work has been featured in 60 anthologies, chrestomathies, textbooks and readers.
E: poemleto@gmail.com

MOTHER

Translated from the Serbian original by Novica Petrovic

Point of departure Rijeka
destination Miločani
means of transport a Willys jeep
the welcoming committee
confused by the arrival of a white-skinned bride
in uniform
asked in unison if she spoke our language
their house is a castle
stone upon stone up to the sky
a Turkish observation tower
and then the myth about the prince's gift
received after a battle
and a victory of course

The fair-haired grandfather
his eyes as blue as the sea
which he never got to see
when he felt a sharp pain
under the ribs
he would mount a horse
and disappear into the mountains
what was that daughter-in-law that his son
brought like
a short-haired Amazon
speaking a different tongue
who sleeps with a revolver
under her pillow
and asks
what is to be found behind that hill
another hill and behind that one
a hill
and behind that one

Lois Baer Barr
USA

Lois is a retired Spanish professor who currently volunteers as a literacy tutor. Her work has been published in England in the *National Flash Fiction Day Anthology (2020)*, as well as in the *Chicago Tribune*, and in Venezuela at *Letralia*. Thrice nominated for a Pushcart Prize, she was a finalist for the Rita Dove Poetry Prize and won Poetica's chapbook contest in 2013. Her second chapbook of poetry, *Tracks: Poems on the "L,"* is forthcoming from Finishing Line Press.
E: loisbaerbarr@gmail.com
W: www.loisbaerbarr.com

WISHBONE
For Ethel Cooper Baer (1924-2012)

Fingers sticky with matzo meal and egg
form another orb dropped into the pot
that sinks then bobs to the top, simmers
with a dozen balls in eddies of fat.
You wipe the sweat from your upper lip,
leave a smudge of dough on your cheek.
Cover pot, rinse hands, look at the clock,
light a smoke.

Screwdriver and hammer in hand, trowel
in red clay. You pull tomatoes ripe from vines.
Fingers reach octaves, feet barely reach pedals.
Mozart sonatas soar through the house,
curses echo off the fallboard when you flub
an arpeggio.

At thirty you learn to drive, so we're off.
Rainbo Bread bags in your fists, we clamber
downhill. Swans, ducks, geese welcome us.
You lead the way to Cave Hill Cemetery's.
secret cave.

Vines thick with yellow and white blossoms.
You leave green caps. Pull stamens slowly
out the back; drops of nectar fall on our lips.
You can catch more flies with honey, you say,
but your tongue lashes my detractors. You teach
me names of wildflowers and bird calls; never
to sew or iron.

Simmering chicken permeates the air.
Your hands slick from pulling meat off the bones.
Wiping the slender clavicle on your apron,
you extend one side. Our thumbs touch the apex.
We tug. Crack. I get the bigger side. The wish.
I always got the wish. I wish you'd gotten
more wishes.

Tayane de Oliveira
GERMANY / BRAZIL

Tayane is a 27 year-old Brazilian writer residing in Berlin. She has been writing since she was 13. She writes poetry, short histories and music. Her work is very personal and sensitive, often dark and melancholic, but at times romantic as well.
E: taycristinepso@gmail.com

SEASONAL JOY

Don't call me friend
Don't call me daughter
Leave it for the my weekend laughter
Shape reality your own way
Just because you were taught, doesn't mean it is right
Lying by my side
Your lie affects me no more

I cried tears of joy when I leave you
I won't go back leaving this way
I won't fall down in that trap again
You are not replaceable but won't be missed

Come, my weekend delight
It's time to give me my seasonal joy
I can't wait for the time to arrive
And take my mind away
From this miserable period
And the profound endless grief
I've never meant to achieve

Open your eyes
Poor naive mind
Your innocent thoughts have poisoned me
And I recall every night
The time of my life
When I thought I had no power
And you broke my heart

I've been dying in the inside
But still would like to heal
I've been crying in the dark
But I need you anyway

Djehane Hassouna
USA / EGYPT

Growing up a few steps away from the Egyptian pyramids and the mysterious world of the pharaohs, Djehane received her BA in French, her MA in Comparative Literature and, at 62 years old, earned her Ph.D. in Romance Languages and Literatures. Despite her struggle with Parkinson's disease, at the age of 76 she also published her first book of poetry, *Rainbow of Emotions*. Djehane is multicultural and speaks five languages: French, English, Arabic, Italian, and Spanish. Her creativity knows no bounds, and she plans to continue writing poems, as well as publishing many more books.
E:djehane@gmail.com
W: www.djehane-poetry.com
FB: @DjehanePoetry
Instagram:@ DjehanePoetry
Twitter:@DjehanePoetry
Goodreads: @20994286.Djehane_Hassouna
Allpoetry.com: @DjehanePoetry

MY GRANDFATHER

Like a time machine, his picture brings back
The years and the days; it also brings back
The conversations and the sweet reminiscences.
The patience of my grandfather knew no bounds.
Encouraging and appreciative, he listened for hours
To my complaints, to my hopes and dreams, to a
Future we envisioned together. I trusted him and
He believed in me. Not once did he blame me as
I poured out my worries and concerns; he never
Told me that I was wrong; he taught me to love
Books and read poetry. Thanks to him, Victor Hugo
Became my teacher and mentor Thus, I turned into
An advocate of the highest moral values that could
Ever be. It's a fact that I was at odds with the rest
Of my entourage who had a different concept of life,
But I felt at peace with myself, and grateful to my best
Friend, my grandfather, who left me with a legacy of
Knowledge and cherished memories, providing hope
As well as guidance during a bumpy and merciless life!
My grandfather was a gentleman by all accounts!

Cathy Hailey
USA

Cathy earned an AB in English at Duke University, North Carolina, and an MA in English, with a concentration in Professional Writing and Editing, at George Mason University, Virginia. She teaches as an adjunct lecturer in JHU's MA in Teaching Writing program, and previously taught high-school English and Creative Writing. She serves as Northern Region Vice President of The Poetry Society of Virginia; facilitates a reading and interview series, *Virginia Voices*; and organizes In the Company of Laureates, a biennial reading of poets laureate held in PWC. Her writing has been published in: *The New Verse News, Poetry Virginia Review, The Journal of the Virginia Writing Project, Written in Arlington, Stay Salty: Life in the Garden State (Vol. 2), Poetry for Ukraine, NoVa Bards, Confetti, The Prince William Poetry Review, Gridpoems*. Her chapbook, *I'd Rather Be a Hyacinth*, is forthcoming from Finishing Line Press in 2023.
E: haileycp@gmail.com
FB: @cathy.hailey.5
Instagram: @haileycp
Twitter: @haileycp

MY MOTHER DISCOVERS WORDSWORTH

She says she never knew, but over fifty years ago,
she must have heard me repeating the same lines
over and over again, *I wandered lonely as a cloud,*
though my dad introduced me to Wordsworth's poem.

Last night, she read it on Facebook and raved
about its beauty, not unexpected because she loves
daffodils, gardens, and nature. She planted patches
out front when she first moved in over forty years ago,

and they bloom every year though their yellow has faded.
When she insisted I read the poem and see for myself
how beautiful it is, I told her I knew it. I'd memorized
and recited it in Brownies when I was seven or eight.

As I worked on memorizing, I learned new words–
jocund, pensive, perhaps vales, bliss, and solitude.
I learned how contractions could be used to subtract
a syllable. I wonder if I counted all the lines and realized

some lines contained an extra beat. I earned a badge—
poetry, oral communication, recitation, I don't know—
but I do know I would sew it or ask Mom to sew it
onto my sash and wear it proudly, a pride still felt today.

I remember the scene of the performance—standing atop
a picnic-table stage at a Girl Scout campground, struggling
to project my voice in the cold outdoors under the shelter
where later we'd roll out our sleeping bags, try to sleep

for a few hours, a challenge after whispering ghost stories,
roasting marshmallows, eating S'mores around the campfire.
May Wordsworth keep Mom's heart, and my own, *fluttering
and dancing* in the *jocund company* of Spring's daffodils.

Craven L. Sutton
USA

Craven is a retired businessman. He grew up in the agrarian environment of eastern North Carolina, and earned a degree in English Literature from UNC-Chapel Hill, North Carolina. Through four decades in the arena of business, Craven sustained an appreciation for the English Romantic Era poets. Since retirement, he has written more than 500 poems, primarily in four collections: *Songs of Innisfree, The Anne Mariah Series, Collected Poems*, and *O Ancient Light – songs of praise and worship.* Each of these works reflects an affinity for musicality in poetry.

E: cravensutton@gmail.com
FB: @Craven L. Sutton

BRING BACK THE TIME

By the fire, children reading,
In your arms, infant feeding,
In this room - a special place –
Things that time cannot erase.

Glow of sunlight in your eyes,
Open windows to the skies;
By my side, you stop and stand,
On my brow, your gentle hand.

Busy now, the hands I see,
Hands that always comfort me,
Hands at work throughout the day,
Hands that brush my cares away.

Hands that held our children near,
Hands that dried their every tear,
Hands that cooked and hands that sewed,
Hands that, always, kindness showed.

Hands that held the Good Book near,
When the unknown brought its fears,
Hands that clasped each day to pray,
Hands that helped me find my way.

Beauty, in those hands, I see,
Showing love so easily;
Beauty, in the touch I feel -
Memories, to me, so real.

Feel your touch upon my face,
Feel the warmth of your embrace;
Memory, bring back the time,
When Mariah's touch was mine.

First published in *The Anne Mariah Series*.

J. J. Steinfeld
CANADA

J. J. is a poet, fiction writer, and playwright and lives on Prince Edward Island, where he is patiently waiting for Godot's arrival and a phone call from Kafka. While waiting, he has published 23 books, including *Misshapenness* (Poetry, Ekstasis Editions, 2009), *Identity Dreams and Memory Sounds* (Poetry, Ekstasis Editions, 2014), *Madhouses in Heaven, Castles in Hell* (Stories, Ekstasis Editions, 2015), *An Unauthorized Biography of Being* (Stories, Ekstasis Editions, 2016), *Absurdity, Woe Is Me, Glory Be* (Poetry, Guernica Editions, 2017), *A Visit to the Kafka Café* (Poetry, Ekstasis Editions, 2018), *Gregor Samsa Was Never in The Beatles* (Stories, Ekstasis Editions, 2019), *Morning Bafflement and Timeless Puzzlement* (Poetry, Ekstasis Editions, 2020), *Somewhat Absurd, Somehow Existential* (Poetry, Guernica Editions, 2021), and *Acting on the Island* (Stories, Pottersfield Press, 2022).
E: jjwriter@eastlink.ca

HEARING A LIFETIME OF WORDS

You have so many versions of your father's last words
a file on love and mortality
from the poetic to the philosophical
from the prophetic to the absurd
a lifetime in a sentence or two
a message to self and son
sad shame you were elsewhere
hearing a lifetime of words.

You go a full week without listening to the news
using the daily newspaper only as a scratch pad
ears and eyes given over to childishness
then you resume your news-following routine
third item on the morning news: *world has ended ...*
but you have already gone through that
and you imagine smiling
like a mayfly given an extra day.

You begin to accumulate last words
when the extra day has gone
always tricked and cheated
another day denied
sweet music silenced
that's the way it goes
blunder and artifice sanctified
you try out still another version
for yourself and your father
and the world that you love half of the time.

From *An Affection for Precipices* (Serengeti Press, 2006).

Maryam Imogen Ghouth
UNITED ARAB EMIRATES

Maryam holds a BA Hons in Communications, Authoring, and Design from the UK. She is of Saudi Arabian, Iranian, and British origin and lives in the leafy suburbs of Dubai, where she makes poetry films that explore psychological themes such as belonging, shame, and existential crises. Her *Journey of Becoming* series was showcased in Dubai's arthouse cinema, Akil, in celebration of female artists. Under her recent initiative *#mcollabs*, she invites directors and musicians to fuse their art with her poetry. She wrote and narrated a poem for *Under the Sun*, a short film directed by Alla Dulh, which is premiering worldwide, and another poem for *Liked by the Crowd*, an art film directed by award-winning film director Pegah Ghaemi. Her most recent work focuses on written poetry, deriving inspiration from nature and science, with her latest appearing in *Vita Brevis Anthology* and *Sky Island Journal*. Maryam's first chapbook is forthcoming.
E: maryam@maryamghouth.com
W: www.maryamghouth.com
Instagram: @maryamghouth
YouTube: @maryamghouth

MY AUNT THE PIRANHA

Her teeth grow sharper when she speaks,
and her words interlock without breath
like the jagged rows lining her jaw.

She hurts.

Sometimes
I want to feed her to a river dolphin or a heron,
and be done with her bites.

Instead, I summon her flaws
to draw her in like bait,
then inculpate.

But to whom do I assign fault?

If the piranha is the self
and the Amazon River is the brain,
do I blame the Amazon River on the ocean
and the ocean on a meteorite?

Shakti Pada Mukhopadhyay
INDIA

Shakti has been published in a number of international magazines and journals including: *Borderless, Passager, Molecule, Better Than Starbucks, Tatkhanik, The Dribble Drabble Review, The Poet, Deep Overstock, MindFull, CafeLitMagazine, Down in the Dirt, Academy of the Heart and Mind, Indian Periodical*. His writings have also been accepted for publication in *Muse India, Scarlet Leaf Review*.
E: shaktimukherjee.synbank@gmail.com

ETERNAL MOTHER

Her sweet smiles I cherish in mind,
like the shining stars at night I find.
My first teacher she was with skills rare,
to teach me with personal care.
With her help, I was cool
to get my entry in a school.
My mother she was, with a heart
that taught me, never to hurt.

To take my first breath, who helped me?
By whose help, my learning steps I could see?
Like the 'Lady with the Lamp', who sat on my sick bed?
Who was my best cook? And with me who played?
When the gale had rushed to the dale,
 to come home fast, who did tell?
Whether she belongs to "Maxim Gorky" or mine,
eternally she is supreme divine.

When father used to reprimand,
behind my mother I could stand.
When things had gone wrong,
with a kiss or hug, she helped me to stay strong.
When I was about to fall,
like a cushion she was to my beck and call.
Bringing joy, she was like the spring
to nature and her offspring.

When the wet breeze flows in rains,
my heart sings with her remembrance.
In the evening, when the Moon does smile,
my Mom whispers in my mind for a while.
All her sorrows were hidden in a safe,
forever which remained as a waif.
Remembrance of her face with a drop of tear,
makes my heart slit with despair.

The vermillion on her forehead
made even the midday Sun red.
To give my teens for a glance,
may she come once?
With motherland, she is synonymous
and is superior to Heaven to us.

Bill Cushing
USA

Called the "blue collar" poet by classmates at the University of Central Florida because of his years serving in the Navy and later as an electrician on commercial and naval vessels, Bill returned to college at the age of 37, earned an MFA from Goddard College and taught at East Los Angeles and Mt. San Antonio colleges for over 23 years. A nominee for both a Pushcart Prize and Best of the Net, Bill was named as one of the Top Ten Poets of L.A. His poetry has appeared in numerous journals, both in print and online. His book *A Former Life*, published by Finishing Line Press, was honoured by the Kops-Featherling International Book Award. He also won the 2019 San Gabriel Valley Chapbook Competition with *Music Speaks*, which medalled in the 2021 New York City Book Awards. His latest chapbook of poetry, *. . . this just in. . .* combines poetry and images. Bill is currently finishing up a memoir focused on his years working on ships in both the Navy and afterwards.
E: piscespoet@yahoo.com

THE PRODIGAL FATHER

Somebody told me
how you had grown
as a man worthy
of honour on your own.

I wasn't there,
avoiding the weight
of giving you due care
forcing you to live enate

as I surrendered
to another life
that was false and rendered
me to live like one who'd died.

Now I come to you
to be absolved,
hoping to mask or subdue
a lifetime uninvolved.

Published in *A Former Life*, poetry collection.

Mathews Mhango
MALAWI

Mathews is an Internal Auditor by profession working in the public sector. He likes to write poetry on different issues that affect society.
E: mhango798@gmail.com

YOU

I always feel loved and my life is worth living because of you
At my weakest point the strength to keep on going comes from you
When the tears fill my eyes, the one to dry them up is you
At times when am lonely, the one is longing to embrace is you
In that quite time, the one to whisper that lovely thought in my ears is you
Sometimes situations make me sad and the only one to brighten my face is you
And when I lay down and sleep, I want to dream about you
I know when I will wake up, the one to greet me with a beautiful face is you
I know the family that holds my hand when I fall is you

Sanda Ristić-Stojanović
SERBIA

Sanda graduated in philosophy at the Belgrade Faculty of Philosophy. She is the author of 15 poetry books, and one of four authors in the joint collection of poems, *From the Shadow of the Verse* (Gramatik , 2012). She was an editor in the publishing house "Beletra", editor-in-chief of the literary magazine *Kovina* (KOV, Vršac), and her poems and short stories have been published in numerous anthologies and collections of contemporary literature. She is a member of the Serbian Literary Society, the Association of Serbian Writers, and the Aesthetic Society of Serbia.
E: sandastojanovic@yahoo.com
FB: @sanda.risticstojanovic

PASSION AND SADNESS

(Brother)
Translation Sonja Asanović Todorović.

The star draws
A man at the table.
The sun roars like his blood.
The sun signs his hardest thought.
The night parades
in the profile of his longing.
A hard thought of the day
yet toasts
the bending of his grief
over sorrow and passion
of the growing Sun.

Robert Beck
USA

Robert currently resides in New York City and worked in theatre and video for many years. His short stories and poetry have appeared in a number of print and electronic publications.
E: robert1beck@yahoo.com

REMEMBERED

Beverly and Arlene,
flame-haired sisters,
beloved cousins,
your presence still
sears my heart's core.

They of gracious heart:
treasures who couldn't last
beyond their brief time,
causing empty spaces
in passing so soon.

They left no offspring
to console us for their loss,
nor trace of loving smiles
carried down the timestream
to offer some continuation.

Lingering memories,
sweet fading images
captured by old cameras
will be a lost remembrance,
after I am gone.

Amrita Valan
INDIA

Amrita has a master's degree in English Literature, and has worked in the hospitality industry, several BPOs, and also as content creator for deductive logic and reasoning in English. She writes poems, essays and short stories, which have been published online in: *Spillwords, ImpSpired, Potato Soup Journal, Portland Metrozine, Poetry and Places, Café Lit, Café Dissensus, Modern Literature* and *Indian Periodical,* as well as in several international anthologies.
E: amritavalan@gmail.com
FB: @amritavalan

HANDS THAT CARED

Pale fragile lady
Ladyfinger tapering
Trembling fingers squeezing juice
Lemonade fresh,
For tired daughter
Come home from school.

And the bent tarnished bangles
Bronze and gold glinted sunlight
Of her care
And the darker iron band
She brandished symbolising
Strength of her bond with my father, strong as
Iron, hinting tough love and
Loyalty,
Endurance, that stands the test
Of time.
My mother, who brought me into
Our family
And showed me its height
And stature.
Quiet and stately, in humble service
Without grand gestures.
Yet I remember the loving fingers
Stiff with arthritis quiver slightly
As she squeezed out the juices
For my lemonade of love.

Betty Naegele Gundred
USA

Betty lives in Grass Valley, a former gold-mining town in the Sierra Foothills of Northern California, and has enjoyed writing since high-school when she was editor of her school's literary magazine. She received her B.S. from Cornell University and her M.S. from Michigan State, and taught middle-school science for 20 years. After retirement she has been able to devote more time to her first love, poetry. Her work has appeared, or will soon appear, in publications including: *Current, The Heron's Nest, Frogpond, Last Leaves, Months to Years, Orchards Poetry Journal*, and *Open Door Magazine*. She is currently writing a series of memoir stories.
E: bettynaegele@gmail.com
FB: @bettynaegelegundred

THE THISTLE

It seemed a fitting gift for you, Mom
a silver pin, souvenir of Scotland's flower,
the thistle,
the lavender bloom, an amethyst,
your birthstone.

Back from my travels,
you passed before I could give it to you ...
no matter now,
the trinket forgotten.

Later, I wondered
if you would have worn it –
in the grip of crippling pain,
in the fog of dementia?

Perhaps in truth
the pin was meant for me,
a reminder,
that you were the sparkling gem,
the flower trapped in thistled thorns.
I keep it still.

Suzan Alparslan
USA

Based in Los Angeles, Suzan's poems have been published in several journals including: *Poeticdiversity, Poetry Pacific, The Voices Project* and *Smartish Pace.* She holds an MFA in poetry from Antioch University, and was a proud mentor at *writegirl.org.*
E: suzanalparslan19@gmail.com
Instagram: @suzeyed

SWIMMING WITH AUNT BEA

In pristine pools we waded, bounced and floated
always as guests of time. The most recent *you* took
buoyancy assistance from assorted, friendly bendy tubes.
You'd mount them like a child onto a carousel
pony whose tempo magically mirrors her own.
Slow motion is expected in the water,
so there, you kept no one waiting.

The friction of this world left your limbs swollen.
Father's belt and boarding school beatings had you
pointing your own finger down your throat, over
and over, over time. But in the pool, the burden
vanished upon contact, like the crisp sound
of mallet to bell. It was just you, the sun
and the LA holy water.

I'd swallowed a glimmering strand of your mythology
early on, and a new exotic ease took root. Trees
decked with oranges and lemons ripe for plucking
tempted a new kind of December onto my New
York-child eyes. Your solar-powered instinct lured
me in. Tanned breast and backstrokes, so devout
as they sculpted the fluid space, and you.

The salon-blond mane and face-stealing shades
were their own art of thirst, quenchable (it seemed)
by a 1:1, pool to sun. When I was thirty-five,
and you were seventy, my grey skies had become
opaque from steeping in my own fallout-ash.
So, I swam for 3,000 miles, swam in
my own gunk, straight to your sun.

And we went deep in our saline bubble *at the club,*
glided through man-made blue in that manicured plot
where polished men swing clubs. Beneath the glassy
surface you became a vast terrain of shadowy
depressions and sunspot destinations. And, beneath
your surface I could see accumulated pain; proof
of time's promise to wean us off these vessels.

And the pool salved our crossover, familial scars.
You pointed out that *this* was the only time
when I would be *exactly* half your age.
And the pool held our secrets. There seemed

infinite dips and submersions ahead, endless
waves of memories blushing to the surface,
reserved only for aunties and their nieces.

Sometimes we'd slip in at the golden hour and just
wade there like a lullaby until the sun set off to sleep.
The neuropathy set in deep, your legs defeated
like unwelcome immigrants. Your steps' only request
to sense the ground: denied. On our last swim,
I noticed a bee floating, lifeless but in motion,
flirting with the suction at the gutter drain.

Then the club closed down. No floating allowed,
not even for Beas. Then came no touching,
not even my hands on your stiff shoulders.
Then came un-homed words not making the distance
to your tongue. Then came the inside-water
filling tired lungs. Then came the un-fun tubes,
not made for floating.

For the first time in 400 years, Jupiter overtook Saturn
in the *Great Conjunction*. I joined other distanced
and masked, half-faces to witness the celestial olympics
in an *old-is-new* kind of December. The surge
of saltwater rose and spilled out from my face holes. I
could taste it, even before the dreaded call came in.
A foreign knowing in my 5am-body,

that you had slipped out from under me like a loose
tectonic plate, and left me wading, lost in the debris. My
ever-constant planet, dear Aunt Bea. I sense some current
has swept and fed *you* back to the infinity sea, outside
of this chronic gravity and the somatic need for cool relief.
I close my eyes open and feel you there, where
the *buzz* also returns to, after having been a bee.

Margaret Clifford
AUSTRALIA

Margaret began writing poetry after her retirement from full-time work. She has self-published two collections: *Stitched Pages* (2016), and *Layers of Life* (2019). One of her poems, *No Words*, published in *From the Ashes* edited by C.S. Hughes (2020) has been exhibited by filmmaker, Lori H Ersolmaz, and has received international acclaim. Margaret's poems have been published in journals and magazines worldwide, and are regularly used for reflection in liturgies.
E: mdkanga@gmail.com

SKETCHING HOME

Can you sketch your childhood home? a Grand Girl asks. It should be easy, I say. All those family scenes etched deep into my memory.

A fire glows
through the open grate
warms the smoky kitchen
as we gather
at first light, sipping sweet, milky tea
before scurrying off to morning chores.

Mum clothes us
with her love,
prompts stories beyond her patch
as she strings the beans,
checks the homework,
equitably portions the milk pudding.

Dad demands
silence at the family table,
saucers his tea, teases the toddlers,
assigns farm chores
then escapes to the bedroom
with his cough and crossword puzzle.

We quarrel
over "turns" to wipe up,
refine the art of whip-crack with tea towels,
rush to the outhouse to avoid tasks
praying the resident snake
is asleep.

We feel the warmth
of each other's presence
across the rows of beds along the verandah
and as the roof thunders and leaks
we dream
our futures into being.

It's all still there playing out in time. But I can't sketch it or capture its homeness without those who lived and loved and made it home.

Jean E. Ragual
SINGAPORE / PHILIPPINES

Jean has worked in Singapore as a domestic helper since 2008. Her work has been featured in the Migrant Workers Photography Festival 2019, and she won the "Places and Architecture" category. She was also finalist of Migrant Worker Poetry Competition, Singapore (2017), and overall winner AIDHA Unspoken Life Photography Competition (2020). Her story, *Behind Our Smiles,* was published in *Call and Response 2*, and her poem, *Restore Their Freedom* published in *The Tiger Moth Review Eco Journal Issue 5.*
E: jeanragual@gmail.com
FB: @100015462605963

FORGIVE ME CHILD

The mother is the light of home
A mother, who has a big role in the family
A mother, who will do everything
As a mother I need to find a job
It is hard to me to leave you
But this is for you

My child forgive me, if I am far away from you
Forgive me, if I left you at your young age
Someday you will understand everything
Thank you for all your stories to make me happy
When I talk with you
You give me strength everyday

Forgive me, Child
If you wonder why
Our home is not already complete or
Why you never see your father already

You are my only strength, my inspiration to continue our dreams
You are my treasure that GOD gave to me
Not all I can give to you
But I do everything I can, to make you happy
My love for you is forever

And no one can replace in my heart
My child, you are my flesh and blood
You are the reason I am strong and brave
While I am far away from you

Forgive me, my child, I love you forever

Caila Espiritu
PHILIPPINES / HONG KONG

Caila is a Contemporary English Studies graduate. While she has been writing privately for some time, she has only recently begun publishing and submitting her work for contests. Verbalizing her thoughts as a quiet and reserved person can be challenging, but she finds her way around it through poetry, dancing and photography.
E: cailaespiritu@gmail.com
FB: @caila.espiritu
Instagram: @cai.exp
Instagram: @arcai.vz
YouTube: @Caila623

THE REUNION

Every now and then, I set foot within
The gentle, loving arms of these four walls.
Their faces dating back to who-knows-when,
My ears perk up as distant voices call.
A line of generations stand in front
Of me. We were once separated by
Vast seas washing us up with tides so blunt.
Now we stand hand-in-hand, and eye-to-eye.
A breaking news reported over food.
The sweet aroma of *Pandesal* buns.
The crunch of roasted *Lechon* sets the mood.
On the side, drunk karaoke shot-gunned.
> They'll come and go. The next time? No one knows.
> But today, blood is redder than a rose.

Stephen Ferrett
SCOTLAND

Since an early age, Stephen has always had a passion for writing and poetry, and has recently published his first children's book, with a sequel on its way.

E: stephen.ferrett@mottmac.com

BROTHER

Come stay with us
Do as little, or as much as you want
Words, such incredibly special words
Spoken with such sincerity, bring tides of relief through endless streaming tears.
Emotions that have been held back for years.
Words that are better than "I love you"
More exciting than any childhood Christmas memories at the age of two.
A bond between me and you, from the same, special genetic two.
Incredibly close, unwaveringly tight, a brother's intimate words, harbour shards of soulful and heavenly light
It's now my time to utter the same line.
Come stay with us, stay with me and mine.
Gather strength and peace through uninhibited healing time
Rest your tired body, soothe your aching mind.
Let us repay your love, in some small way in kind
Brother, my beautiful Brother, come stay, I pray.

Ed Ahern
USA

Ed resumed writing after forty-odd years in foreign intelligence and international sales. He's had over 300 stories and poems published so far, and six books. Ed works the other side of writing at *Bewildering Stories*, where he sits on the review board, and manages a posse of six review editors.

E: salmonier@aol.com
FB: @EdAhern73
Instagram: @edwardahern1860
Twitter: @bottomstripper

LEGACY

The shuffling feet of those ahead
tramp a dust-clouded pathway
in which I just see and touch
the backs of those still living
and hear the wind-blown murmurs
of those gone further beyond.

The ever-fainter bobbing heads
have concocted my making
and conditioned my soul.
No matter how I turn
or twist away from them
their march is ever before me.

For will it or not
I am always of them,
Swaddled by ancestors
who mostly know me not,
staring ahead as they shuffle on,
never looking back.

Theresa M. Lapensée
CANADA

Theresa is a poet and writer finding her way back to words after a 20 year business career. Recent poems have appeared in *Lived Collective* and *Open Door Poetry Magazine*. She believes poetry is a vehicle for truth, and must come from the heart.
E: wordsfortheheart.ca@gmail.com
W: www.linktr.ee/wordsfortheheart.ca
FB: @wordsfortheheart.ca

SISTERS

It's the ones with the sorest throats
who have done the most singing
and it's the ones dancing to Elliott Brood
on a hot summer night
who stay connected across continents

Our parents did teach us this

Laughing with you about complete nonsense
equals pure joy
I am holding your hand wherever I am

Victoria Milescu
ROMANIA

A member of the Writers Union of Romania and PEN Romania, Victoria graduated the Faculty of Philology, University of Bucharest, and worked in education and the press. She writes poetry, literary chronicles and children's literature, and has had a large number of books published, both in Romania and internationally. Her poems have been translated and published in several international literary anthologies including: *Voices of Contemporary Romanian Poets, Doamnele poeziei/ The ladies of poetry/ Les dames de la poesie, On The Wallaby Track. A Journey Across Memories,* and *anthologie de poésie roumaine contemporaine/ Contemporary Romanian Poetry Anthology.*
E: victoriamilescu@yahoo.com

A KIND OF FAMILY

My father is the sun
and my mother is the moon
it's a glorious family, isn't it
I am a white dwarf star
that's happened
my older sisters are famous and beautiful
they have families called constellations
I am alone, I'm an anonymous
I hope, however, that an earthling astronomer
fond of his work
will discover me and give me a special name
looking at me through the telescope every night
full of curiosity or even of love
for something unusually
I can't ever see him
but I know he lives on a beautiful planet
which mom and dad take care of
I can't get close to him
he can't climb up to me either
I'm little but my love is as his marvellous planet
which I can't touch it, for I shall die.

Marilyn Longstaff
ENGLAND

Marilyn was born in Liverpool, and has spent most of her adult life based in the North East of England. The daughter of Salvation Army Officers, whose vocation meant a nomadic existence, she is a member of the writing, performing and publishing collective Vane Women. Her work has appeared in a number of magazines, anthologies and on the web, and has written five books of poetry. In 2003 she received a Northern Promise Award from New Writing North, and in 2005 gained her MA in Creative Writing from the University of Newcastle. In 2011 her book, *Raiment* (Smokestack Books), was selected for New Writing North's Read Regional campaign. The poems for her latest pamphlet, *The Museum of Spare Parts* (2018 Mudfog), came from her involvement in Stemistry, a University of Newcastle Public Engagement project, devised and run by Lisa Matthews to consider creative responses to modern genomics. Her other books are: *Puritan Games* (2001, Vane Women Press), *Sitting Among The Hoppers* (2004, Arrowhead Press), and *Articles of War* (2017, Smokestack Books).
E: marilynclong@aol.com
W: www.vanewomen.co.uk
FB: @marilyn.longstaff.9

YOU
For my daughter

There you are in the military-green hospital wrap,
a red head screaming at the interruption of being born;

shock of hazel eyes and sad mouth in the playgroup portrait,
silver-sand hair cut in a mullet by the child-minder's children;

saucer-smiling in front of the half-demolished shed,
in your Dad's old rolled-up cords and size 8 boots.

A child who didn't want to read and loved running.
I'm late and worrying I won't recognise you –

although I know you better than I know myself,
I know you not at all. Ridiculous – of course it's you,

your tall assurance, easy style in men's Top Shop faded denim,
stripy top and flip flops – in winter,

and your open grin as you give me a hug, say 'Oh my God,
I've just got some men's white linen trousers

and had to try them on in the men's changing rooms'.
I speculate about how we've both been mistaken for men

with our broad shoulders, narrow chests, long legs, confidence,
as you talk about things I'll never comprehend

and drink banana milk shake with cooked dinner,
in Café Neon.

First published in *Raiment* (Smokestack Books 2010).

Francey Jo Grossman Kennedy
USA

Based in Georgia, Francey taught at Slippery Rock University, and Emory University, both Alma Maters. She plays Beethoven and Mozart, loves the ocean, and paints the sky. Her chapbook is titled *Acorn Rain* (2020), published by Finishing Line Press. Her poetry appears in: *Georgia State Review, Adanna, Artemis, Green Ink Poetry* among others.

E: kfrancesjo@yahoo.com

THREE AM CALL TO BIRTHDAY TWIN
For James

brother twin
over the miles asleep
I call you
please wake to find me
seeking solace
with my spinning thoughts
turning names
your name says
"He will wake for you"

birthday child many years ago
gift brother to me
brown eyes like mine
----- are they grey green
Just eyes filled with all they see
I call you
in pretence of checking on you
but so surely in need

only far off philosophies
distinguished such real and true
no matter here
your voice
I hear sleepy
but with quiet words
Hello, I'm glad it's you
Hello, I'm trying hard to be glad
it's me too
brother mine

Aishwariya Laxmi
INDIA

Aishwariya holds a master's degree in communication, and is a writer, editor, blogger and poet. Her poems appear in *Spillwords, The Drabble*, anthologies by Sweetycat Press, Writefluence, Soul Poet Society, ThirdEyeButterflyPress, Indie Blu(e) Publishing and others. She was featured in *Who's Who of Emerging Writers 2021,* by Sweetycat Press, and was one of the TOP 3 winners of High-5 - The Great Poetry Hunt Contest, organized by WriteFluence. She has also written flash fiction and essays, and has written and edited for greeting card companies, e-learning companies, MNCs, start-ups, newspapers and advertising agencies.
E: mymewse@gmail.com
W: www.aishwariyalaxmi.com
W: www.ash.fambase.com

FAMILY TIES

I come from a nuclear family
It's just my mom, my dad and me
My relatives are scattered worldwide
There's a cousin in Philadelphia,
another in Muscat
One in New Jersey and
yet another in Connecticut
Seven years ago, we all met in person
And someone gave a PowerPoint presentation
On our family tree of five generations
Over six thousand ancestors in all
We have a WhatsApp group
And periodic meetings on Google meet
Where we chatter endlessly
I'm grateful to them
For enriching my life and supporting me

Mariana Mcdonald
USA

Mariana trained with Al Gore in 2019, and joined the international Climate Reality Leadership Corps. She is a poet, writer, scientist, and activist. Her work has appeared in numerous publications including: *Crab Orchard Review, Lunch Ticket*, *The New Verse News, About Place Journal, So to Speak*, *Cobalt, Longridge Review* and *InMotion*. She co-authored *Dominga Rescues the Flag,* with Margaret Randall, about Black Puerto Rican heroine Dominga de la Cruz (Two Wings Press, 2020). She was named a fellow of Georgia's Hambidge Arts Center in 2012.

E: maricmcd@yahoo.com

SISTER

If I could touch you through the skies
I'd make your sorrows end,
with balm of hope and memory.
I'd make these two your friends.

If I could hold you across the years
I'd bid the clouds embrace
your freckled shoulders, dab the tears
to tidy up your face.

If I could find you past the dark
I'd twirl a vibrant light
— a universal strobe —
to bring you into sight.

If I could turn time inside out
And make tomorrow spin,
I'd whirl the galaxy we'd be
sisters once again.

TS S. Fulk
SWEDEN / USA

Born in Ohio and raised in Amish country TS S. Fulk, a neurodiverse English teacher and textbook author, lives with his neurodiverse family in Örebro, Sweden. After getting an M.A. in English literature from the University of Toronto, he taught English at the Czech Technical University in Prague. Besides teaching and writing, TS S. is an active musician playing bass trombone, the Appalachian mountain dulcimer, and the Swedish bumblebee dulcimer (hummel). His poetry has been (or will be) published by numerous presses including: T*he Light Ekphrastic, The Button Eye Review, Enchanted Conversation, Journ-E: The Journal of Imaginative Literature, The Red Ogre Review, Perennial Press, Lovecraftiana* and *Wingless Dreamer.*
E: tssfulk@gmail.com
Instagram: @tssfulk_poet

JUST FOUR DUCKS ON A POND

Nuclear family
two parents, two children
always harmonious
with bright smiles they gleam
like mallards on a pond
Instagram tells me so

My landmine-filled home is nothing
like those idyllic pastorals
that others post and boast about
instead we just try to survive
Yet there are ripples on the lake
hinting at some disturbances
hiding just below the surface
distorting their calm reflections

As a burnt-out parent
I empathize with the mallards

Mary Keating
USA

A graduate of Yale Law School, Mary is a Pushcart Prize nominee, and has been published in several journals and anthologies including *Scribes*MICRO*Fiction, Wordgathering, Santa Fe Writer's Project* and *Poetry for Ukraine*. Mary writes on a variety of topics, and after becoming a paraplegic as a teenager, she found poetry a great way to raise awareness of how disabled people are treated.
E: mmarywords@yahoo.com
W: www.MKeatinglaw.com
Twitter: @MaryKeatingpoet

SIX YEAR OLD GIRL AT SUNDAY MASS

I'm stuffed into a pew at the Church
of the Resurrection of Our Saviour Lord Jesus Christ
with my two older sisters, my baby brother,
my dad and my mother. Our yellow Lab
Heather's stuck home alone. She isn't allowed
which makes me wonder if she'll be allowed
in Heaven when Jesus comes again.

My sisters and I sport matching yellow
shifts with scenes from Barbados
stitched on in bright threads
Mom and Dad got them there
last year on their annual vacation.
Mine's really short now and my thighs
are sticking to the wood.

We rushed to 10:00 o'clock mass.
I barely had time to dress
before Dad yelled: everyone in the car
in 2 and 1/2 minutes. I forgot
to put on my underwear.

I hope no one notices—
just keeps staring ahead
at my two older sisters
with their shiny blonde hair
not me with dull brown.

I look around and wait
for the priest to tell us
what to do: kneel, stand, kneel,
sit down. If we get it right
we must go to Heaven.

Mom turns and smiles. She's two
sisters away—her beehive hairdo's
caved in on the side she sleeps
despite her silky pillowcase.
I keep waiting for a bee to buzz
out of her hair at any moment—
some miracle to stop

the endless drone. The priest
raises his hands for us all

to stand and my skin smarts
as the wood pulls me back
as if a devil's hiding inside the oak.

I let out a small yelp
which makes me wonder about
Heather home alone
waiting for us—or the milkman—
but it's Sunday and the milkman
isn't coming today. When we stand

my shift rises up. My sister
Anne pulls it down whispering,
"Did you forget something?"
I turn red. She starts to laugh
which isn't allowed in Church.

Soon all us, even Dad
are trying not to, squeezing
our eyelids, scrunching
our faces biting, our lips
crying, except, of course
Mom mad as a queen bee.

We sit and kneel and stand
in endless repetition and
when Mom's eyes aren't stinging
me, the wood devil is, and I'm secretly
praying Heather wouldn't be allowed
in Heaven because Mom's going
to kill me and I'm going somewhere else.

Bhisma Upreti
NEPAL

Bhisma is a poet, essayist, novelist and translator. He has published 21 books featuring poetry and essays/travels, as well as a novel. His books have been translated into English, Japanese, Serbian, Farsi, Hindi, Sinhala and Turkish, and his works into Korean, Slovenian, Russian, Tamil, Kannada, Chinese, Malay, Macedonian, Cambodian and Bengali. A gold medallist at the National Poetry Festival organized by Nepal Academy, Bhisma is also the recipient of awards including: SAARC Literature Award, Gopal Prasad Rimal Rastriya Kavya Puraskar, Uttam Shanti Puraskar and many more. He has represented Nepal in many international literary forums and festivals, and is the secretary of PEN Nepal.
FB: bhisma.upreti

WHAT IF THE SKY FALLS?

My little son asked me -
'Papa, what if the sky falls?'
I first looked at him
and then to the sky.

For me the sky is a faith
a pure faith,
For me the sky is a belief
a firm belief,
For me the sky is an aspiration
a tall aspiration,
For me the sky is a heart
a big heart.

I've been drenched with the downpour from the sky
I've run overjoyed seeing rainbow in the sky
I've seen the moon and stars in the sky just like my own children
and loved them eternally
I've found the sun blazing in the sky
and written a song of light.

The thoughts abound in my mind
I alternately look at the sky and my son
and become speechless
how to answer his question.

My little son asked me -
'Papa, what if the sky falls?'

Biman Roy
USA / INDIA

Biman, an India born American poet. He is a psychiatrist by profession, and has been writing poetry for more than three decades. Widely published, Biman has been nominated for Best of the Net and Pushcart awards. He is the author of one chapbook of prose poems, *Of Moon and Washing Machine*, (Uncollected Press), and two other poetry chapbooks: *Dinosaur Hour,* (Finishing Line Press), and *Navigating the Quartz Forest* (Author's Reputation Press).
E: bimanuma@gmail.com

ORPHANHOOD

I was raised under the shadow of my grandma,
who struggled under the shadows of teak and deodar
         to keep her grandson unhurt.
Then came the pain of separation.

I started growing under the shadows of scaffoldings,
bridges, holding rivers and stern voices of strangers
and parents, who were there and not there.
(One predicted her death accurately and the other
remained a distant voice on the phone.)

Then you came like tax-free water and air,
         tending me tender as a plant and showing me ways
to free myself from *myself*.

And life, being life,
played its own tune—

sometimes like Bach,
sometimes like The Beatles.
When you left,
I became an orphan for the third time,

         maybe for the last.

Published in *Sorrow has a weight of its own.*

Claudia Recinos Seldeen
USA / GUATEMALA

Claudia is a first-generation Guatemalan American currently residing in Western New York. She is the author of the YA verse novels *To Be Maya* and *Catch Me if I Fall*, and her poetry has appeared in *The Amphibian Literary Journal* and *MONO*. When not writing, she's flying through the air on a trapeze.
E: ccr002@gmail.com
W: www.recinosseldeen.com

4 A.M.

There are worse fates than this.
There is no worse fate
than this.

The muffled wail
like a siren.
Threading me out of sleep.
Plucking my heart
into my throat.

The restlessness that
awakens
as I make my sleep drunk stumble
down the hall.

Freedom is just around the corner.
Freedom has abandoned me
forever.

And all the while
the window
ushers in
a square of moonlight.

There are worse fates than this:
My feet
worrying the carpet like
whipped dogs.
A little hand
hot in my own.
The
beat beat beat
of the ceiling fan.
The pattern of shushing sounds
I make
like a foreign language
as I lull my child
back
to sleep.
As I lull
myself
back
to sleep.

This
slow-faucet
drip
of minutes.

This unspooling
ribbon
of hours.

It will end.
It will never end.

But,
there are worse fates than this:
A head
resting against my breastbone.
Little mouse wriggles.
The stillness.
The stillness.
The somnolent
feather beating
of my heart.

Is it still
my heart?

It will be, one day.

(It will never
be mine
again.)

Anamika Nandy
INDIA

Anamika hails from Digboi, Assam. By profession she is an educationist. She loves to write poems and to express her emotions in words, and enjoys working towards the development of a better society.
E: anamika.sweety1431@gmail.com

MY BLACK AND WHITE FAMILY

Waking hours of mine,
Pass amidst the black and white.
Disseminate myriad hues ol life,
They stimulate my body and mind.

With them I take a flight,
To 'Xanadu', 'Hogwarts' and the like.
Sometimes I sprightly dance,
In the jocund company of 'Daffodils'.
Sometimes I sing,
Like the 'Solitary Reaper'.
Sometimes be candid like 'Lizzy',
Sometimes empathetic like 'Candida'.
Infuse in me at times,
The fiery spirit of 'Draupadi',
To fight 'The Tempest' of life.
Make my eyes brim with tears,
When death wallops ,
The virgin love of 'Laaila -Majnun' -
the great lovers of all time.

The enlightened ones,
Aspire my mind.
A sea of knowledge,
Sousa in me, well and wide.
What profound peace,
I draw from them !
Words do fall short,
To express them.

In weal and woe -
Always by my side.
Close to my bosom,
They do forever reside.
My best of cronies,
My pillar of strength,
I do bide happily,
With my black and white family.

Jill Sharon Kimmelman
USA

Jill is a two-time Pushcart Prize-nominee in Poetry (2017 & 2021), and Best Of The Net nominee (2018). Publication credits include: Vita Brevis Press, *Spillwords, Fine Lines, Better Than Starbucks Poetry & Fiction Journal, Poetic Musings, ILA Magazine*, Prolific Pulse Press, World Inkers Network, *Garden of Neuro, Writing In A Woman's Voice*, PLCS, Eric Publications, and Sparrow Productions. Jill has contributed back cover text to international themed anthologies, as well individual books, and her debut collection, *You Are The Poem*, is a unique, 3-themed collection, poetry art book.
E: jskimmelman@icloud.com
FB: @jskimmelman

FOR JACK FROM YOUR JILL

You live inside my heart
whisper sage wisdom every day
my imagination soars as never before
spiralling beyond all earthbound dreams

You longed for my happiness
for your daughter's sweet smile to return
your compass, a father's pride
to find the perfect man to learn who I am
adore me, worship me, as you did me in turn

Somehow you knew just how it would unfold
from love-driven desire, you envisioned it all
where the dance would lead us, how the chips would fall
this tale of love unveiled itself just as you foretold

First you had to find him, not an easy task
then to understand his journey
anticipate the questions only you knew I would ask

Education, profession, each met your highest bar
yet gave no hint of challenges ahead
would he make your dreams his own
make me his shining star

Surely you had doubts
he had to be a man of honor, my kindred spirit
what exactly was this guy all about?

A man of the backwoods, his camera never far
images of forest paths, midnight starry skies
you searched deep within his soul
sought to embrace the lamentation
of his plaintive cries

His heart was but a satchel for his unheard pleas
along with prayers, plans, schemes
hope lived on, it flourished
emboldened by his dreams

Living each day within love's tapestry
basking in its golden glow
like fine wine, a love enriched by age
as Yeat's poems, each more beautiful

when we turn the page

We are pieces on life's board of chess
each move an answered prayer
delivery of dreams
once I was your very own princess
now I am his newly-crowned queen

You would love him Dad, be proud to call him son
his love is true, he treasures me
like the rare gem you always said I am

If only we could, though we can never go back
what an extraordinary gift it has been
to be the Jill to your Jack

When my time is nigh
I know I will not be alone
for you will be there waiting
arms open wide to embrace me, re-claim me
joyously welcome me home.

CELEBRATION OF A LIFE, AS YOU REMEMBER HER
For Pratibha

Now
you are the one reaching for
your daughter's jam-smeared little hand
laughing aloud & louder with glee
leaving your footprints
large & small on endless beaches of
pristine white sand

Remember swimming together
in azure waters of summer
the taste and scent of ripe mangoes
your school recitals she never ever missed

Your beloved mum
lost to you … far too soon
a voice that knew every word to
Good night Moon   .

She is still here, she is everywhere
you need not look far or wide
she is the scented breeze that brings the night
in dreams is where she holds you tight

She is smiling at you from pictures hung
on crowded walls
you can hear her precious voice ring clear
beneath your daughter's laughter

Is that not perhaps be the sweetest sound of all

Tell her stories at the table
pass them on as cherished gifts

Choose not to mourn this parting
embrace instead a treasure trove
a million mixed memories
delivering smiles & tears
recalling shared celebrations
throughout those too-few joyous years.

Emmanuel Chitsanzo Mtema
MALAWI

Emmanuel is committed to social change through teaching adolescents in High School. He also serves humanity by writing poetry and Christian devotions. He has one publication to his name titled: *Kasupe Devotions Volume 1,* and has his poems widely published locally and internationally. His work usually reflects on topics of love, identity and societal belief systems. Some of the publications his work has appeared in include: *A New World Anthology, LOCKDOWN 2020, On the Road Anthology (Vol. 2), Childhood (Vol. 2), Walking the Battlefield Anthology, The Scarlet Anatomy, BNAP 2019 Anthology, Scribble magazine*, *ACE World Magazine, Trendy Magazine (2nd and 3rd Issue*) and *Nthanda Review.* Two of his poems were translated into Spanish and were published in the *Libero America Journal.*
E: mexarly@gmail.com

ANGOZO

'My son, watch and learn;'
From the mighty Achilles
One that walked this earth in our time
The slaying of the Trojan prince
He made us win against poverty
Giving it a wound that would not heal
While he fishes us out, one after another
Into a land filled with opportunities
And making his breastplate our shade.
Mkamwini, yet too much Valour
One would mistake him for *mwinimbumba*
From how he was holding the house together
Mutu omodzi uwu unkasenza denga ndithu
Not a day existed where he pleaded for respect
As is the tradition of alleyway thieves,
Nonetheless many emptied gallons on him
Anointing his feet with honour
For a warrior that he was;
Extraordinarily fearless and skilful
You would think he had superhuman strength
Angozo; a man of few words

Anna Dunlap
USA

Anna unwittingly followed Rilke's advice to "wait and gather sense …
for a lifetime" before attempting to write "ten good lines" of poetry.
After a long career in public education policy and corporate
communications, she is now writing poems while making time for
family, friends and philanthropy. Anna's poems have been published
in several anthologies including: *An Uncertain Age* (Ink Sisters Press,
2022), *Support Ukraine* (Moonstone Press, 2022), *Doctor Poets and
other Healers* (Golden Foothills Press, 2022), *Spectrum 31: Well
Done* (Spectrum Press, 2022) and *Poetry for Ukraine.*
E: amdunlap1@msn.com

SHADES OF HOME

Mom was fond of green in the pale shades –
said it was a comfort in the swelter of Florida

with its prickly palmettos, strangling moss
rows of cinderblock houses built on hot sand.

She wore mint-coloured blouses, wrap-around
skirts, fed the family on melamine plates

of eau de nil, purchased with S&H green stamps.
Seafoam flowed from her knitting, needles

angled against despair, clicking to rhythms
of the unborn, of too many mouths.

She bought a yard-sale sofa in hushed sage
made pillows to match, a place for Dad

to land, to rage as he failed to make a go of it
in the Land of Opportunity, rockets & orange juice.

I keep her mementos in a red silk box –
ring of emerald, postcards from kin

a baby's sweater & bonnet, knit for me
in the colour of a pale spring leaf.

Alicia Minjarez Ramírez
MEXICO

Alicia is an internationally renowned poet, translator, singer, university professor, and radio and television broadcaster. She has won numerous awards including: The Prize for Cultural Excellence 2020, awarded by the government of Peru, The Nobel Laureate Kobi Rabindranath Tagore Award (India, 2019), The Excellence Prize in the World Poetry Championship (Romania, 2019), the Literary Prize of unpublished poetry *Tra le Parole e L'infinito*, *20th edition* (Italy, 2019), and many others. She was awarded an Honorary Doctorate granted by the International Forum of Creativity and Humanity I.F.C.H (2019, Morocco), the EASAL medal by the European Academy of Sciences and Letters (Paris, France, 2018), and many others including winner of a special mention medal in the International Poetry Prize NOSSIDE (Italy, 2015), recognized by UNESCO.
E: minjarezalicia@yahoo.com

I BELONG TO YOU
To my beloved husband.

I belong to you ...
From the faint shade of acacia
To the roots of the sun.
As a star falls
In constellated emptiness,
Kissing tulips that sing
Naiads of the road.

I belong to you ...
As subtle wave of silent music
In a night of silvery foam;
Like prophetic stardust
Invades the ivy's deliriums,
Spreads its smiling foliage,
Requires - desists
Sap, fruits, essence and moon.

Am I word, zephyr and world in your gaze?

Dr. Rehmat Changaizi
PAKISTAN

Rehmat is an international poet, writer and philosopher, with multiple awards to his credit. A graduate in Medicine and graduated in Law from M.I.U. Azad Jammu & Kashmir, he is the Chief Operations Officer at Soflay Inc, and the author of poetry books: *Mia Bella Dea, Bella Diosa* and *Ma Belle Déesse*. He is Chief Editor of the yearly international poetry anthology *Whispers of Soflay*, and Chief Editor of *Soflay Anthology of Microstories*. His poems have been translated into French, Spanish, Chinese and Arabic, and have also been published in several journals, magazines and anthologies at both national and international level.
E: rrehmat@aol.com

YOUR LOVELY FACE
To my wife: A.M.R.

Your love tides
Arouse in my heart ocean
When see your lovely face

Your existence
Discover the ways of love
Emotions hold dainty place

Then light spread in beauty dale
Two lovers disappear in
Their rainbows mend together
And the dance of pleasure start
Meteors glow everywhere

Time is smiling
It knows the cosmos secrets
How life hovers on the rise

And my lips stride
Try to adhere nectar brims
When see your lovely face.

Srimayee Gangopadhyay
INDIA

Srimayee is a 23 year-old poet from West Bengal, currently pursuing Masters in English Literature. For Srimayee, poetry is a means of introspection, a dive into nostalgia, and connecting with self. She started writing poems at the age of 11, while searching for enigma in the ordinary, and as a mechanism to uncover her introverted self. She critiques films on various e-platforms, and interprets works of eminent poets/writers.

E: srimayee98@gmail.com
FB: @srimayee.ganguly.3

PERIWINKLE
Dedicated to my mother

When peals of mirth swell the breeze,
Undulating me in the wildest of dreams;
Daylight peeps into the hidden corners
Cradled in the verdure arms of eternity.
Lift me up the ground, higher and still higher up!
Swirl me 'round in circles till I'm forced to lie still;
Till the whirlwind of your love leaves me in a haze, and then-
I'll rest my sleepy head upon your gentle knees.
Send me to the little haven where our joys untouched-
Reel me to where your harmony rehearse the way I heal-
I know you'll always be there, mother, making me bloom;
In a clandestine harbour, my homeland by the sea.
You let me get the best of each moment with you;
You were there to push me on my loving swing,
I love you forever more for giving me your eyes,
For kissing my teardrops into dewy edelweiss.
I can never forget the way your fingers stroked my hair,
Or the way you made me believe-
Oh yes, you made me believe, dearest mother!
In true love, magic and fairy-tales-however unreal they may seem.
With each new step, I stride, unto the esplanade of my dreams,
As roads, seasons and people- they all keep changing;
Yet only one remains for you and for me-
A periwinkle in the palm of your hands
And a little amethyst that conjured my lilac dreams.

Judy Jones Brickner
USA

Based in Wisconsin, Judy has found that the pandemic has provided the luxury of having all the time in the world to write poetry. Her poetry has been published in several local magazines.
E: jlbrickn@wisc.edu

THE LEONA GENE

Her Christmas decorations ranged from
tacky winter sleds made of popsicle sticks
glued together, to quite marvellous creations
of crocheted starched angels and
tiny wicker baskets filled with miniature
balls of yarn with a hat pin strategically
stuck through. When our children came
home from school with a macaroni necklace
or a glitter bomb picture, we lovingly joked
that they must have inherited "the Leona gene."
Her outlet was always the busy home seamstress
making clothing for plus size women, doing
alterations, sewing clothes for us four kids,
knitting, crocheting. She lives on in the memory
of crafts, patchwork quilts, baby blankets.
Surprise overcame me one May in the drug store
selecting a large, frilly Hallmark—only to remember
she no longer needed a Mother's Day Card.

Rose Menyon Heflin
USA

Rose is a writer and artist living in Wisconsin. Her poetry has appeared in numerous journals and anthologies spanning four continents. It won a Merit Award from Arts for All Wisconsin in both 2021 and 2022, and one of her poems was choreographed and performed by a local dance troupe. Additionally, she had an ekphrastic creative non-fiction piece featured in the Chazen Museum of Art's Companion Species exhibit. Among other venues, her poetry has recently been published, or is forthcoming, in: *Abyss & Apex, After..., The BeZine, Deep South Magazine, Defunkt Magazine, Fireflies' Light, Hare's Paw Literary Journal, Isotrope, Moss Piglet Zine, Of Rust and Glass, OpenDoor Magazine, Pamplemousse, Poemeleon, Red Weather Literary Magazine, San Antonio Review, SPLASH!, W.E.I.R.D. Magazine, Witches Mag*, and *Xinachtli Journal* (Journal X).

E: rosemenyonheflin@gmail.com

ODE TO MAMA'S OLDSMOBILE

I always wondered
just what became
of my mother's old baby blue Olds.
Outdated when I was a small child,
it's the earliest car in my memory.
It was a veritable boat,
and it must have been a 455
or some other Rocket because
I used to love the way
that piece of V-8 marvel
would fly around the country backroads
every weekend.
It didn't have A/C,
so we would roll down the windows,
the wind whipping through our hair,
on roads no cop would waste time on.

I vowed to have a car just like it
when I grew up,
but my lead-footed Mama
quickly disabused me of that notion,
wanting more for her little girl.

When she showed up to pick up
from school one day
in something small and white,
I howled with pain
and sobbed endlessly.

Now I live in a city,

where it is too much of a hassle to drive,
so my halcyon days
of soaring down backroads,
the fresh air tickling at my nostrils,
the wind blowing tangles into my hair -
days I had naively assumed were infinite -
are sadly, regrettably, gone forever,
just like my Mama's old blue Olds.

Ermira Mitre Kokomani
USA

Ermira is a bilingual poet, essayist and translator. She has published poetry, short stories and scientific papers in Albania and the US. In 2021, her book of poetry, *The Soul's Gravity,* was published in Albanian. Her poetry has appeared in: *Jerry Jazz Musician,* (New York, 2020), *Sequoyah Cherokee River Journal 7*, (October, 2020), *Live Encounters*, (December, 2020), CAPS book *Mightier-Poets for Social Justice* (New York, 2020), and in international anthologies including: *Musings during a Pandemic, I Can't Breathe* (Kistrech Poetry Festival, Kenya, 2020), *Rutherford Red Wheelbarrow 13*, (New Jersey, 2020), *A New World*, *Mediterranean Poetry 2019*, Montclair Write Group anthology, *NJ 2018*, Brownstone Poets anthology, and a range of other print and online publications. Ermira has also translated from Albanian into English the fiction novel, *The King's Shadow,* authored by Viktor Canosinaj. She has majored in English Language, and has taught writing in NJ colleges for some years. She works for Rutgers University libraries, is a member of Montclair Writers' Group and Red Wheelbarrow Poet, and regularly reads her poetry in Open Mic events in New Jersey, New York, and France.
E: emitre1@yahoo.com

PREGNANT MOTHER

Dedicated to my daughter Mariela Mitre in her first pregnancy

Expecting, nurturing the embryo inside you,
growing the human dimensions to infinity,
bringing mother-son souls closer,
bonded inextricably in eternity.

Madhavi Tiwary
KINGDOM OF BAHRAIN / INDIA

Madhavi's first rendezvous with writing was at college where her scribblings - which she fondly called 'poems' - were proudly and regularly passed on to like-minded class mates. It then took a decade for her to pick up writing again with zeal and zest. As a result, in the past few years, she has written over 50 articles and editorial columns, and has written as many poems, many of which are still hatching in the warmth of her private closet.
E: madhavi.dwivedi@gmail.com

A SUSPENSEFUL COURTSHIP

This story needs to be written
of a boy and a girl
who looked the other way for forty years
kneaded, blanched, cooked, savoured
their passing years,
gave their heart to some
and then took it back
ventured with their hopes or
squashed some dreams
played to the gallery of life,
collected some accolades
binned some memories.
Each was a book
with a million characters
each was a treasure trove
with colossal collections
each was a coffer
with some dead dreams.

And then those forty years melted
they stood stunned
in one frozen moment.
Will this moment thaw and
carry them to the shore
or will it just desert them back
in the sea of their lives?
Time will tell …

Zev Torres
USA

Based in New York City, Zev is a writer and spoken word performer whose work has appeared in numerous print and on-line publications including: *NYC: From the Inside, Poetry is Dead, The Rainbow Project, My Father Taught Me, Escape Wheel and Suitcase of Chrysanthemums from Great Weather for Media,* Three Rooms Press' *Journal of Contemporary Dada Writing and Art*, and *Friend and Friendship*. Zev has featured at many New York City spoken word venues and, in March, 2022, participated in POETS BUILDING BRIDGES: A Worldwide Triangulation Project for World Poetry Day.
E: zevtorres@hotmail.com

CONSANGUINITIS

While the storms raged,
Branches snapped,
Floors quaked,
Channels flooded.
The entire house rattled.
Dishes crashed to the floor.
Thunder overlay thunder,
As if several storms,
Proxies for an endless war,
Converged.

We buffered each other from the terror,
Learned to speak,
To comfort,
Our words responding to words,
Yours to mine,
Mine to yours,
Not to the specifics or the content.
But to the flow,
To the tender back and forth . . .

~~~

And now? Where are you?
Still pushing back?
Seems you've learned to pick your spots.
Good for you.

~~~

We have much in common:
Our diffuse politics defying normative trends although
We never see eye to eye;
Our inexplicable craving for leafy greens —
Arugula, watercress, red leaf lettuce.
Even gave you a head of kale
As a house-warming gift,
When you returned from your missions
To Cali and Ouagadougou,
And bought an apartment

Five zip codes to the east.
You remember what happened next,
Don't you?

You grabbed the kale,
Wrapped like a bouquet of flowers,
Took a bite off the top.

~~~

Hints of them
Your mother, your father,
Must inhabit me as well.
Different traces than are present in you.
Speaking with authority —never came naturally to me.
My defense mechanisms are more refined.
Or muted.

~~~

["Your mother", "Your father":
Our own nomenclature].

~~~

A story you love to tell
One of your standards.
"How are you two related?"
Someone once asked.
"We have the same parents" you said,
So proud of yourself,
As if you had stumped them with
A Wymanesque kinship imbroglio [@1993].

~~~

During those storms and for years after,
You were much more like your mother.
Reactive, combustible.
Displayed those shades.
But you never reacted well when someone pointed out that
You and she shared those traits.
So we learned to avoid those topics.

Avoidance: a side-effect of growing up.

~~~

But now, you are more like your Dad,
The way you speak: with authority,

Obliterating any doubt that
You could possibly be mistaken.

Like your explanation for why
Two negative numbers when multiplied together,
Always yields a positive result.
Your analysis made no sense,
But you must be correct because you
Expounded on it with
Steadfast bravado.

~~~

Remind me,
What it was that you did or said,
That drove me to slap your phone
Out of your hand,
Onto the floor,
In front of your mother.
"I hope your father saw what you just did,"
She — your mother — usually not appreciative of
Subtle ironies or given to
Flashes of spontaneous humour – said.
Of course he did.
He was there too,
Laying in bed, in the hospice,
The room still chilled
By his last breath.

Acton Bell
USA

Acton Bell is the pen name of Vasti Carrion. She started to write poetry and short stories when she was 10 years-old, and won a fairy tale contest for her first short story *Witcherell*a. Her teachers always encouraged her to write and she became a several times published poet. She was a member of all-women writing groups *Writegirl* and *Words of Womyn, and* occasionally attends open mics events in Los Angeles.
Contact details witheld.

MOTHERS ARE MOTHS

Mothers Are Moths,
Within the months,
Attracted to the light of motherhood
progressing each month,
biting moth holes
In the paper of calendars
moths into a lamplight.
a lamplight---
where babies are warmed
within light
and incubated
beyond seven months
premature births,
give birth to maturity
and the immaturity
of infants,
the heartbreaks
of a womb--
when your heart
is nestled in your womb,
the pain
the doubt,
whether you are birthing
life or death.
The artificial incubation:
a technological bird nest
maintains life of
a pre-mature newborn
and the emotional
intelligence of Mothers
who experience this.

Shakhzoda Kodirova
UZBEKISTAN

Shakhzoda is a 15 year-old aspiring poet from Navoi, in south-western Uzbekistan. From a young age she was fond of literature, and, at age just seven, she began to read books and study oriental literature. Her poems and stories have been published a number of magazines and newspapers in Uzbekistan, as well as in Germany, the USA and Belgium. She is an ambassador of Iqra Foundation – teaching the children of today for a better future.
E: shahzodaqodirova007@gmail.com

MY GRANDFATHER'S GARDEN

My grandfather has a garden,
Massive and beautiful.
The fruits are ripe,
It is delicious and sweet.
My grandfather will take me
To the Garden when I go.
He tells a lot about the garden, The legends.
I really like Grandpa's stories.
Captivating, meaningful, Each verse.
The fruit that my grandfather planted,
The trees are fruitful.
Beautiful from each other, Fruits are very colourful.
My grandfather knows the secrets of every tree.
He knows how to look after them.
The trees are also very familiar to my grandfather.
Talk to my grandfather, Have a good conversation.

END

FAMILY Vol. 1 – contains 91 contributions from 88 poets in 26 countries worldwide: Albania, Australia, Bosnia & Herzegovina, Bulgaria, Canada, China, Cuba, England, Georgia, Hong Kong, India, Israel, Jamaica, Malawi, Mexico, Nigeria, Philippines, Republic Of Ireland, Romania, Saudi Arabia, Scotland, Serbia, Singapore, Singapore, Slovakia, and across the USA.

www.THEPOETMagazine.org

Printed in Great Britain
by Amazon

83372056R00129